WHO AM I NOW

Also by Sirshree

Spiritual Masterpieces - Self Realisation books for serious seekers

The Magic of Awakening : 111 Answers on Life and Living
Answers that Awaken: Access the Source of Wisdom within You
100% Karma : Learn the Art of Concious Karma that Liberates
100% Wisdom : Wisdom that leads you to experience and be established in your true nature
You are Meditation : Discover Peace and Bliss Within
Essence of Devotion : From Devotee to Divinity
Dip into Oneness : Beyond Knower, Known and Knowing
The Unshaken Mind : Discovering the Purpose, Power and Potential of your mind
The Supreme Quest : Your search for the Truth ends there where you are
The Greatest Freedom : Discover the key to an Awakened Living

Self Help Treasures - Self Development books for success seekers

The Source of Health: The Key to Perfect Health Discovery
Inner Ninety Hidden Infinity : How to build your book of values
Inner 90 for Youth : The secret of reaching and staying at the peak of success
The Source for Youth : You have the power to change your life
Inner Magic : The Power of self-talk
Self Encounter : The Complete Path - Self Development to Self Realization
The Five Supreme Secrets of Life : Unveiling the Ways to Attain Wealth, Love and God
You are Not Lazy : A story of shifting from Laziness to Success
Freedom From Fear, Worry, Anger : How to be cool, calm and courageous

New Age Nuggets - Practical books on applied spirituality and self help

The Source : Power of Happy Thoughts
Secret of Happiness : Instant Happiness - Here and Now!
Excuse me God... : Fulfilling your wishes through the Power of Prayer and Seed of Faith
Help God to Help You : Whatever you do, do it with a smile
Ultimate Purpose of Success: Achieving Success in all five aspects of life
Celebrating Relationships : Bringing Love, Life, Laughter in Your Relations
Everything is a Game of Beliefs : Understanding is the Whole Thing

Profound Parables - Fiction books containing profound truths

Beyond Life : Conversations on Life After Death
The One Above : What if God was your neighbour?
The Warrior's Mirror : The Path To Peace
Master of Siddhartha: Revealing the Truth of Life and After-life
Put Stress to Rest : Utilizing Stress to Make Progress
The Source @ Work : A Story of Inspiration from Jeeodee

WHO AM I NOW

Beyond mindfulness into no-mind

SIRSHREE
Author of the bestseller *The Source*

WHO AM I NOW
From mindfulness into no-mind

By Sirshree Tejparkhi

© Tejgyan Global Foundation, 2016

All Rights Reserved.

Tejgyan Global Foundation is a charitable organization with its headquarters in Pune, India.

First Edition	:	April 2016
First Reprint	:	October 2016
Publisher	:	WOW Publishings Pvt. Ltd., Pune
Printer	:	Vikram Printers Pvt. Ltd., Pune

Copyrights are reserved with Tejgyan Global Foundation and publishing rights are vested exclusively with WOW Publishings Pvt. Ltd. This book is sold subject to the condition that it shall not by way of trade or otherwise, be lent, resold, hired out, or otherwise circulated without the publisher's prior written consent in any form of binding or cover other than that in which it is published and without a similar condition including this condition being imposed on the subsequent purchaser and without limiting the rights under copyright reserved above, no part of this publication may be reproduced, stored in or introduced into a retrieval system, or transmitted, in any form, or by any means, electronic, mechanical, photocopying, recording or otherwise, without the prior written permission of both the copyright owner and the above-mentioned publisher of this book. Any person who does any unauthorized act in relation to this publication may be liable to criminal prosecution and civil claims for damages.

To those seekers
who have the thirst
to reach and abide
in the true self.

CONTENTS

	Preface	9
	Introduction	13
1.	Enquiry about Enquiry	19
2.	Enquiry of the Mind	39
3.	Enquiry of the Self	59
4.	Guidelines for Self Enquiry	71
5.	Enquiry in the Now	85
6.	Ending the illusion	105
	Epilogue	121
	Appendix - I	129
	Enquiry About God and Beliefs	131
	Appendix - II	159
	About the Author and the Foundation	161

 **PREFACE**

Sometime around 1917, an author had said, "When you give a man a book, you don't give him just twelve ounces of paper and ink and glue—you give him a whole new life." However, this book does not give you life. Instead, it gives you death—the death of the mind. And the death of the mind is the greatest of all spiritual experiences. If a seeker follows the teachings imparted in this book, death of the mind is bound to occur, which as outlined in the following chapters is a precursor to Self realization.

In recent times, the practice of mindfulness has been gaining a lot of momentum. But what exactly is true mindfulness? Is it just observing the breath? Is it watching the body sensations? An often ignored aspect is watching the mind, i.e. the thoughts and sensations, as separate from yourself. Through this book, Sirshree, the author of several books on practical spirituality, teaches a simple yet powerful method of not only watching the mind, but of going beyond mindfulness and dropping the mind. This is done through the power of four words: "WHO AM I NOW?" Whether you are a beginner who wants to learn how to watch the mind or someone who is experienced in meditation, this new technique of asking "Who am I now?" elucidated in this book will elevate your practice to the next level.

Self Enquiry is an ancient method of Self realization in which you ask yourself, "Who am I?" This method had been forgotten with the passage of time and revived by realized souls such as Guru Vashishta and Adi Shankaracharya. Today many have taken to this path after it has been strongly revived once again by Ramana Maharshi in the recent past. However, its finer nuances have again gone missing and it has become one of the most misunderstood of practices. The uniqueness of this book is that it provides the missing links by introducing Self enquiry—with Understanding. This understanding helps you to understand the Self as well as the technique in depth. This in turn enables you to reach the Self easily and definitively. Without this understanding seekers fail to get the desired results.

While "Who am I?" is the question traditionally asked in Self enquiry, "Who am I now?" is another powerful question that further makes the practice of Self enquiry immediate and sharp. With the addition of "now" to the timeless question "Who am I?", Sirshree has enhanced Enquiry of the Self into Enquiry in the Now. With Self Enquiry, you discover your true nature. But, in your day-to-day activities, as you go through various situations and become angry, irritated, fearful, and so forth, you move away from your original essence. At such times, Enquiry in the Now, i.e. "Who am I now?" will help you shift to the present and to your true self. You may have been an angry or a fearful person a moment back. But with Enquiry in the Now, you will be reminded of who you actually are and be led back to your true nature.

This book contains various questions asked by seekers. The answers given by Sirshree demystify the topics of mindfulness, meditation, and Self enquiry, and provide the missing links in these practices. There are three main parts of this book: Enquiry of the Mind, Enquiry of the Self, and Enquiry in the Now. Let this book, step by step, lead you from mindfulness to mind emptiness, from *practicing* mindfulness to *being* in the no-mind state. That's where the illusion vanishes and your true self manifests. So, let's enter the doorway to discover the supreme truth.

...Editor

Whatever is happening,
with whom is it happening?
Is it happening **with** you,
or *for* you?

INTRODUCTION

Once upon a time, a king declared that all the houses in his kingdom would be demolished and then built anew. As per his decree, all the houses were torn down. The people watching it, asked the King, "Our old houses are gone; but where are our new houses?" The King said, "Go and stand before this mirror one by one and you will find your new address. You will then go and stay at the address that you see in the mirror." Each person went and stood before the big mirror. Some found their address, some did not. The ones who did not find their address were automatically transported to a harrowing desert. The ones who found their address were transported to a heavenly palace.

The mirror was the same; then what was the reason that some people reached the desert and others the palace? Why did some people find themselves to be a king or queen in a grand palace? The answer is simple. They saw themselves in the mirror in the right manner. It is important to see yourself in the right manner and identify your true self. Then the question is: How to see yourself in the right manner? Do you see yourself as a 'limited individual' or do you see yourself as 'the unlimited Self'? When you see yourself as separate from the trinity of the observer, the observation, and the observed—that's the right way to see yourself. The art of seeing yourself is what you have to learn from this book.

When you see yourself in the right way, you can achieve liberation from the cosmic illusion. Some call this state as Self realization, while others call it *moksha, nirvana, samadhi, kaivalya, mukti,* etc. All these terms are given to the same state, which is the state of *being*. This state too is called by different names such as: I-am-ness, sense of presence, Self Witness, Consciousness, etc.

The ultimate purpose of every human being is to attain Self realization and express the qualities of the Self (which is also known as God, Consciousness, Lord, Creator, *Ishwar*, Allah, Witness, Experience of *being*, etc.). The Self is formless and limitless, it's omnipresent and omnipotent. But the characteristic of the Self is that it connects with something and starts believing itself to be that object or being. When the Self connects with a body, it considers itself to be that limited body. Although the body helps the Self to experience itself, but the body also becomes a reason for the Self to forget itself.

The mind is also a creation of the Self. The mind too identifies itself with various beliefs such as: "I am a Hindu/ Muslim/

Christian/ Jew... I am an Indian/ American/ African... I am a son/ daughter/ brother/ sister... doctor/ engineer/ plumber..." If you observe yourself closely, you will discover that you are unconsciously identified with one belief or the other from morning to night. (All those beliefs are merely labels, not the reality.) What's interesting is that people are not even aware of this. But now that you are aware, you have to practice disidentifying and detaching from all these false beliefs. And then you have to start living as your true self, in the experience of *being*.

That experience of *being* is constantly present but we get so busy in our daily activities that we are unable to experience it. Every event of life, whether negative or positive, is indicating: "Whatever is happening, with whom is it happening? Is it happening *with* you, or *for* you?" Learn to go to your experience of *being* in every event.

With earnest practice of questions such as "What is the state of my mind right now?", "Who am I?", and "Who am I now?," your mind surrenders and you learn to live in the present moment and get established in the state of *being*.

In that state, you come to know that the body is merely your mirror. It reflects yourself to you and you are able to experience yourself due to this body. This Self experience is constantly going on. There is not a moment when you cannot experience yourself (the real, formless, universal Self). However, somebody may say, "I cannot experience myself." The reason is that you have yet to understand the truth. That's the missing link. As your understanding of the truth rises, you will start experiencing yourself. You will forget your reality repeatedly and you will be brought back to it again and again. You will be trained to remind yourself in every circumstance who you actually are and to take any decision from that reference point. That decision will be the right decision. Gradually you will develop the habit of taking decisions in this manner. Thereafter you would want to face every problem or take every decision as the *real you*. Then it wouldn't matter where you are—in the examination hall or at home, at the workplace or in the market.

Real life actually begins *after* being established in the real self. Hence, may you get established in the Self. May you start living and enjoying the supreme life.

● ● ●

If you believe
"Everything within my skin is me
and everything outside my skin is not me,"
then Enquiry breaks this belief.

1
ENQUIRY ABOUT ENQUIRY

Q. 1 : I have heard about various paths to Self realization, but which one should I follow?

Whatever be the number of paths, they can primarily be divided into two. Actually there is only one way—Divine Grace. Grace is the only way. But to begin with, we can say there are two paths.

Q. 2 : Which are these two paths?

The first is the path of surrendering. It is also called the path of *bhakti* or devotion. Devotion is acceptance, love and gratitude for God, amazement at the Lord's creations and ways of working. Practices such as chanting and singing praises of the Lord are all part of devotion.

Q. 3 : And the other path, is it that of meditation or service (*seva*)?

Both these practices come under the second path, which is

wisdom. Without wisdom, during meditation or service, the individual is always present who practices meditation or renders service. In other words, once you finish meditating, the mind returns and takes credit for practicing meditation and feels proud. The same is true for service too; the mind becomes more arrogant instead of dropping. An arrogant mind is an obstacle in the attainment of truth.

Who am I? How is everything in this world functioning? How is everything in this world happening automatically? What is the purpose of this drama that is going on? If, through the right Guru, one attains the answers to these questions, one's ego drops. Here 'ego' means the sense of separateness from Self and assuming a separate identity. The moment the ego drops, the ultimate truth manifests. You can call this truth by whatever name—God, Lord, Allah, Self, your true self, Witness, Universal I, and so on.

Q. 4 : I guess *karma* (right action) also falls under the second path, and the same mistake of the mind becoming egoistic can occur in its practice too.

Yes. Till the mind considers itself to be the doer and is mired in false beliefs* and notions, it will always become dominant on performing karma. That is why a Guru is needed, who can break the ego and liberate you of false notions and beliefs. The Guru becomes a medium and provides guidance in dissolving the ego. With the right wisdom, karma can become a great practice to propel one towards Self realization.

---

*Beliefs: You can read in detail about beliefs in Appendix-I of this book.

Q. 5 : **Does the risk of assuming a separate identify also exist in the path of devotion?**

In the path of devotion, there is nothing for the mind to be egoistic about. When devotion is practiced in the right manner, the mind begins to dissolve in devotion. It is the path of constant remembrance and surrendering the separate identity whenever it rears its head.

Q. 6 : **Which path should I follow?**

As mentioned earlier, there is only one path—that of Grace. Let grace unfold and lead you on the path. Pray to attain a Guru, which can happen only by the grace of God. And then you can attain understanding of truth by the grace of the Guru.

When you walk on the path of devotion, you attain wisdom in the end. If you are on the path of wisdom, you attain devotion in the end. *Tejgyan*** has been created to integrate both these paths. To begin with, you can follow the practice of Self Enquiry, which when carried out in the right manner, helps you to attain both wisdom and devotion.

Q. 7 : **Oh! Can you please elaborate further on Self enquiry?**

Self enquiry is a simple and effective practice in which you investigate "Who am I?" However, it is also highly misunderstood. Many seekers practice Self enquiry without

---

***Tejgyan**: You can read about Tejgyan in Appendix-II of this book.

understanding or wisdom. Neither is there continuous remembrance like in devotion. The right practice of Self enquiry includes both 'Enquiry of the Self' and 'Enquiry in the Now' so that both wisdom and devotion can be integrated into the practice.

Q. 8 : But why should I investigate "Who am I?" I know who I am!

You may think, "I know who I am," but that's not so. When an individual identity is assumed in thoughts, it gives birth to the notion of a separate 'I', confined within the boundaries of the human body. With the birth of this illusory separate 'I', whatever happens with the body-mind, seems to happen to a 'me', whatever belongs at the body level becomes 'mine'.

Whatever is inside the skin becomes 'me' and everything else becomes 'not me'. You have been living this lie without questioning it, because you find everyone else around you living in the same illusion.

This illusion is complete when the flip-side of 'I... me... mine' is also *imagined* into existence. Whatever is 'not me' becomes 'you... we... they... it'. This illusion is the fundamental cause of all suffering, struggle, and various defilements such as fear, anger, hatred, ill-will, and envy.

Forgetfulness of who we truly are leads to false identification with who we are not. We have become so addicted with the beliefs and stories that constitute our false personality that we continually try to improve and enrich our personality.

In the competitive world, personality is often used as a mask to flaunt who we are as individuals. But personality is actually a superficial outfit that can be changed. Working on personality doesn't cause any harm unless we believe that we *are* the personality. It is not difficult to notice that no matter how much we work on our personality, we lack the fulfillment of who we truly are.

The mind is a bundle of thoughts in which each thought is linked to a point of reference—the 'I'. No thought can exist without this point of reference. This point of reference called 'I' is a false notion that keeps changing every instant.

Consider an example to understand how the reference of 'I' keeps changing. Suppose one says:

"My hand was injured when I had been to the workshop. I was scared to find my hand bleeding profusely. I thought of visiting the doctor to dress up the wound."

When one says, "I had been to the workshop," the word 'I' is being used to refer to the body. You keep saying many such things throughout the day by assuming yourself to be the body, such as, "I had food, I climbed the stairs, I laughed," etc. Here 'I' refers to the body.

The same sentence also says, *"My hand was injured."* Whom does the 'my' refer to? If the earlier identification with the body were to be used, one would have said, "I was injured." When you say, "My hand was injured," you consider yourself the owner of your body. It is only when you assume yourself as separate from 'your' body that you can say "my hand." Thus, the point of reference for the 'I' has shifted from the body to the owner of the body in the same sentence.

When you say, *"I was scared,"* the 'I' in this context refers to the mind. The body cannot feel scared. The mind feels scared just as it also feels sad or elated, moody or worried.

"I thought of visiting the doctor." Here again, the reference has shifted from the mind to the intellect. Thinking is an intellectual faculty. Here you consider yourself the intellect.

From this example, you can understand how the point of reference is false and how it keeps changing. The use of the words 'I', 'me', 'mine' differs in various contexts. This was an example of only three sentences.

Upon deeper contemplation, you will come across innumerable identities of 'I'. Different identities of 'I' spring into awareness at different points in time. However, due to delusion, you always believe it to be the same 'I'. Being lost in delusion, the real 'I' remains in the dark. Your true nature never gets an opportunity to shine forth as it is eclipsed by these false identities.

Clearing the cobwebs of this illusion requires rigorous and persistent Self enquiry so that you are able to see all the facets of the mind. True enquiry serves the purpose of dismantling this daydream so that truth is revealed.

When you choose to spend time in stillness on a daily basis by focusing on the question "Who am I?" you will be led to the experience of your true self. Asking "Who am I?" or "Who am I now?" is one of the most powerful and effective ways of breaking out of this identification with the false 'I'.

Q. 9 : So, Self enquiry can reveal my true self?

Yes. Self enquiry helps you to raise doubts on the mind, questioning the mind itself—the very mind that raises doubts about the whole world, and questions: Who made the world? When? Where will I go when I die? Why was I born? and so on. But who exactly is asking all these questions from within you? When you ask this question, the mind begins to drop for the first time.

When you conduct Self enquiry and ask yourself, "Who am I?" then this question becomes your mirror. On practicing Self enquiry with honesty and understanding, this question itself can transform into the answer. To reach that state, you need to comprehend the understanding with which you have to ask this question. This is what you have to learn.

When you first begin the quest for yourself, it's like you are sitting on the shores of a lake and looking into the water. You can see the reflection of trees, the sky, the hills, the waterfalls, and everything around. Suddenly you experience a shift and your attention falls upon your own reflection in the water. At that moment all other things cease to be visible and *you* manifest. Although you were there before too and were watching all other things on the surface of the lake, but at that time you had not returned onto yourself. When you shift from everything else and return onto yourself, that's when you witness yourself.

Enquiry of the Self helps you to return onto yourself (the real self, the Self, your essence). The shift that you experience with the understanding of "Who am I?" changes everything, because that's when your body begins to become your mirror.

Q. 10 : Why does the mind drop on Enquiry of the Self?

Let us say you got a thought: "What will happen when I die?" At that moment, if you ask, "Who is it that will die?", then the mind is forced to go within. Within lies absolute stillness (*moun*). In this stillness, death of the mind occurs momentarily. Going within, you discover for the first time that there is nothing that can be called as the mind. What doesn't even exist causes you suffering; isn't that amazing?

That is why it has been called the illusion (*maya*). Illusion means the third entity that seems to appear (but actually doesn't exist) with the combination of two entities. With Self enquiry, you learn to attain freedom from this illusion, due to which the secret of the illusion unfolds and what remains is the sense of wonderment, gratitude, and praises for the Divine.

Let us suppose some flowers are stringed together with a thread. The flowers and the thread are two different objects. But as soon as the two are combined, we call it a garland. Somebody may ask, "Where did the word *garland* appear from?" Just a combination of two objects created a new word —garland. Everybody calls it a garland while using it, nobody says flowers and thread. Have you ever thought about or enquired about this? When there were flowers, there was no garland. When there was a thread, still there was no garland. What happened that a garland appeared? When those flowers dry and wither, we still say the garland dried and withered. Likewise, everybody says that the individual was born and the individual died, but who was the individual? When you conduct an enquiry upon the individual, only then will the secret unfold.

The mind does not have the habit of enquiring about itself. It loves to enquire about everybody and everything else— Why does she do this? Why is that person like this? Why is this thing like that? That's wrong… he's wrong…. But the main point is: who is saying all this? First enquire about this with understanding. You would be surprised to find upon enquiry that there is no individual, there is no mind. There was just a combination of two entities—the Self and the body —due to which the third entity seemed to appear—the mind or the individual. This third entity becomes happy or sad. Isn't it amusing, that which doesn't exist becomes happy or sad!

Q. 11 : What did you say, there is no mind?!

Yes. This is what is called an illusion. The mind is just a bundle of thoughts. Thoughts come together and get imprinted in our memory, due to which we get the impression of existence of the mind. All these thoughts are like waves in the sea. When the waves merge into the sea, the sea becomes calm. Similarly when thoughts liberated from beliefs merge into the absolute stillness (the Self), the mind ceases to be.

Q. 12 : What is my real nature? Is it the same in everyone?

Your real nature is the Universal 'I' or the Universal Self—which is within everyone, and everyone is within it. Words cannot express its nature. But its nature has been described as *Sat-Chit-Anand*. *Sat* means the truth, the Self, the Source. *Chit* signifies the mind. *Anand* means bliss. The Self (*Sat*) created the mind and then identified itself with the mind, thus creating the individual, and then bliss (*anand*) manifested. This is possible in no animal or plant, only in man. Hence attaining a human birth has been considered as the very first grace.

Q. 13 : If I am the Universal Self or *Sat-chit-anand*, then how can I be happy or sad?

When you say, "I am happy," you are assuming yourself to be the mind. However, when you say, "I am happiness," then that's different because you are then assuming yourself to be who you actually are. Till date you have always said, "I am happy." Whenever you are able to accomplish something in accordance with your mind's wishes, you say, "Today I am very happy." Just think for a minute. Have you ever said, "I am happiness"? Maybe not. Because to say so, you will have to go to the experience of Self. You will then feel that this experience is happiness itself. This is because love, bliss, stillness, wonder, creativity, etc. are the attributes of the Self.

Q. 14 : How and when can we attain the Self or the supreme bliss?

Until your world created by your false beliefs disappears, you cannot attain that bliss. The world you are looking at with your tinted glasses does not actually exist; it is just in your imagination.

Try to understand what your false notions and beliefs are and how they get created. With understanding, you will be able to see them for what they are and then they would automatically fall away. If you are assuming a rope to be a snake, then the right understanding will enable you to see the reality. Until you continue to believe a rope to be a snake, your ignorance will not be cleared. Consequently you would be stuck in the cycle of joy and sorrow. This is what has been called the vicious cycle of the illusory world. However, this does not mean that it is enough to be liberated from sorrow. Even joy is a shackle. It is just that sorrow is handcuffs made of iron, while joy is handcuffs made of gold.

Q. 15 : That means beliefs prevent Self realization and stabilization!

Yes. When the mirror (body-mind) gets covered by the dust of beliefs, it is essential to clean it to be able to see your true self. It is only due to beliefs that you consider yourself to be the body and then regard certain things to be a bad omen and some other things to be a good sign. For example, some people believe that itching of their palm means they are going to receive money, a black cat crossing their path is a bad omen, and so forth. All these beliefs are related to the body. These beliefs make the root belief of 'I am the body' even stronger and deeper.

You may have seen a person wearing a costume of a lion or some other animal in an amusement park or at a mall for entertaining kids. Kids look at them in wonder and like to see them and shake hands with them. Now let's think about what is the person inside the costume doing? He is merely playing the role of a lion. If he sees a real cow, will he pounce upon it to hunt it down? You will say, "Of course not! Because that person knows he is not a lion but a human being. He is aware that he has donned the costume of a lion for a short time." Yes, the person knows clearly who he is. He does not forget himself for even a moment and mistake himself to be a lion.

You too need to be totally clear about who you actually are. It doesn't matter what costume you have put on or which role you are playing—that of a parent, sibling, friend, boss, engineer, etc.—you should always remember your true nature. Otherwise one person attacks another who is weaker. People try to snatch things from others due to emotions such as hatred, envy, or greed. If they remember that they have only donned the costume of a human being, they won't get entangled in such things. Hence free yourself from negative emotions and vices. Because only a clean body-mind can become a mirror to experience your true self. The more you get rid of flaws, the better will your mirror become. This mirror will then aid you in getting established in the Self.

The mind is the vessel for all beliefs. Enquiry is for the death of the mind, the mind which we will term as the 'contrast mind'. When this mind drops, it is Self realization. When this mind never rears its head again, it is Self stabilization. This mind with all its beliefs has to disappear.

Q. 16 : How should we begin Enquiry of the Self?

For the right beginning, you need to first understand a little more about the mind.

Q. 17 : What exactly is the mind? Where is it and how does it function?

The mind is just a medium for exchange of thoughts. It is a collection of a multitude of thoughts. The tool of the mind is intellect, which helps us in making decisions. Wherever our attention goes, thoughts of the mind begin in that direction. If your attention goes to a garden, your mind reaches there and thoughts about the garden begin. Thus, the mind is wherever attention is.

Q. 18 : What is the difference between the conscious mind and the subconscious mind?

It can be roughly said that there are two minds inside us. One is the conscious mind and the other is the subconscious mind, which is also called as the inner, intuitive, or instinctive mind. The difference between the two minds is the same as that between air and storm. The work of the conscious mind is visible, while that of the subconscious is invisible. The subconscious mind works quietly, while the conscious mind feels every feeling, thought, and action; and never stays still. The subconscious mind is a combination of memories, intellect, and programming by the conscious mind.

Q. 19 : What is the difference between the (conscious) mind, the subconscious mind, and Consciousness?

The difference is that Consciousness operates the mind. And the mind, with the help of intellect, gives instructions to the subconscious mind and programs it.

Consciousness is like electricity and your body-mind is like a bulb. A bulb cannot operate without electricity. And without the bulb, the electricity cannot express itself as light.

Q. 20 : What is the role of the mind, the subconscious mind, and Consciousness?

All three are required to operate the universe and all its beings. The Self created all three for Its divine play. Just like a dancer needs feet and other parts to dance, in the same way the Self operates through different bodies to continue this cosmic drama. Your ultimate purpose is not to get entangled in the drama and to know that you are the Self. Actually it is your mind that gets entangled.

Q. 21 : How does the mind get entangled?

The mind is such an entity which cannot be seen in the body but we always accept its existence. At this moment if someone asks you where is the mind, the answer is: your eyes. This is because at this moment you are reading with your eyes. In the meantime, your mind went to your brain because it thought about this question but you did not realize it because it is so fast. The speed of the mind is incredible due to which you are unable to catch it. Suppose you are able to read 200-300 words in a minute, but the mind can listen to about 800 words per minute. Hence it brings rest of the 500 words in the form of other thoughts, and that is why you are unable to focus the mind.

For your mind to become no-mind, first your thoughts should reduce. Although the mind can grasp 800 words, it should be content with just one or two words. When the mind attains understanding of the truth, it stops comparing, judging, assuming, labeling, and so forth. The part of the mind that does all such activities can be called as the 'contrast mind'. On attaining the truth, the contrast mind surrenders and drops, and the intuitive mind is free to operate in all its glory.

Q. 22 : Can you please tell me more about the contrast mind?

The contrast mind signifies that mind which compares and judges everything. It splits everything into two—black or white (bad or good), like the contrast control feature of the television or computer. This is the mind that gives rise to fear, worry, envy, insecurity, deceit, assumptions, anger, excitement, and so on. In fact, it is the root cause of all the miseries in human life. It is only present in humans. It is the one that blocks us from seeing the truth.

Q. 23 : How is the contrast mind formed in the first place?

The first thought that arises within us when we wake up in the morning is the 'I' thought. There are variations to this 'I' thought, such as:

- I woke up.
- Now what is the first thing that I should do?
- My eyes are a bit heavy today; is it time for me to wake up?

The words could be different, but all of them pertain to the individual or personal 'I'.

With the advent of the 'I' thought, other thoughts begin to follow. By then, the senses are awake too. It is only after the 'I' thought that the contrast mind forms, which then judges everything as "this was good" or "this was bad". This mind assumes a separate identity for itself and says—my work, my name, my actions, my religion, my country, my sins, my virtues. It compares and contrasts every event, every thought. This is precisely what is sorrow. This is precisely what is bondage. This is what is ignorance. This is what is illusion. This is the obstacle in attaining the truth. This is the black cloud shrouding the sun (Self or the truth). This is what causes the eclipse. This is the speck that has got into your eye and is not allowing you to see even something as obvious as the largest mountain.

The three main functions of the contrast mind are:

a) Breaking : The contrast mind likes to break and see everything in parts. It divides everything in at least two parts.

b) Comparing : After breaking, it then compares the two parts with each other, due to which it always lives in envy and hatred. In order to compare, it constantly sways and churns between the past and the future.

c) Judging : After comparing, it judges the two parts on its scale. After breaking them into good and bad, it thinks, "If this is good, is it more good or less good? If that is bad, is it more bad or less bad?"

In this way, the contrast mind becomes a curtain between you and the Self. When the contrast mind comes to know that it is the one shrouding the Self, it surrenders.

Q. 24 : How exactly does the contrast mind create sorrow?

The contrast mind labels every incident and compares it. Suppose a glass of milk fell down and broke. If you consider this as just an incident, there is no sorrow or misery. But if the contrast mind brings thoughts such as, "Who kept this glass over there? That person has no common sense at all… it was such an expensive glass… such wastage of milk…," these thoughts cause sorrow.

Q. 25 : Can you please explain further about labeling?

Let us understand it with the help of an analogy. You may be aware that machines are used in big companies to apply labels on objects. Imagine you are given such a machine and told that this machine can stick labels to anything. If that machine falls in the hands of children, you know what will happen... they will not only stick labels to tables, chairs, doors, cupboards, they won't even spare people, because they enjoy doing it.

What you have to understand from this analogy is that you actually received a labeling machine in your childhood. This machine is your 'contrast mind', with the help of which you not only stuck labels on yourself, but also on others. It continues to compare between two labels every moment, saying this is good and that is bad, this is more good and that is more bad... In this way the contrast mind applies labels and gives rise to joy and sorrow.

Q. 26 : How can we get rid of these labels?

You can get rid of these labels by asking "Who am I?" With this question, the power of labels begins to wane.

Suppose you get a phone call and you are unable to recognize the voice. In that case you immediately ask, "Who's speaking?" You ask that when you are doubtful. Similarly when you doubt yourself, you look at yourself in the mirror and ask, "Who are you?" This means you suspect that what is seen in the mirror is not the reality. This is an auspicious state.

Now let's understand why the power of labels diminishes on asking "Who am I?" In the example of the phone call, if it was one of your relatives who was playing a joke on you by speaking in a different, made-up voice, then he will start speaking in his real voice shortly after asking, "Who's speaking?" In the same way, by asking "Who am I?" to yourself, the real you manifests in a short time. That is why this question is important.

Q. 27 : I would like to know the process of Self enquiry, but before that, what exactly is the result of Self enquiry? Why should we perform it?

Doesn't every being want peace and bliss? Behind everything you do, isn't it happiness that you seek? Every action you perform is for happiness. But this happiness is lost in the storm of thoughts. And thoughts, whether good or bad, always shroud the light of your true self.

When you are in deep sleep, there are no thoughts. There is pure consciousness, Self, or *being*. Just as a spider weaves a web out of itself and then takes everything back, in the same way thoughts arise from the ocean of the Self and manifest this world. Then these thoughts disappear at night and along with them the world too disappears. This game of cosmic illusion goes on uninterrupted, day after day.

To push aside the curtain of illusion, it is essential to go to the origin of these thoughts. With rigorous, continuous, and repeated Enquiry of the Self, you are able to see all the facets of the mind, in all its colors and forms. As a result the mind weakens and finally surrenders and drops. (The mind will disappear; what never was will become nothing). This mind is the ego. This mind is the false 'I'. Enquiry is for the death of the mind, the mind which we term as the 'contrast mind'. Thereafter your true self will shine forth.

*It is the mind that is sad
and it is the mind that is happy.
Anger, hatred, guilt, fear
— all these are with the mind;
not with me.*

2
ENQUIRY OF THE MIND

Q. 1 : I want to take the path of Self enquiry. But I don't understand it clearly, though I have begun to understand its importance. So, could you please tell me how to begin?

To make this method simple and highly effective, in Tejgyan its process has been divided into two distinct categories: Enquiry of the Self and Enquiry of the Mind. Through this categorization, a major conundrum in spirituality has been addressed. Otherwise many seekers have strayed in the wrong direction because of misunderstanding enquiry of the Self and enquiry of the mind to be the same. There are many courses and activities going on in the world, through which seekers attain knowledge and experiences related to the body or mind, but they are under the false impression that they have attained knowledge and experience of the Self.

Hence it is recommended that the Enquiry of the Mind be practiced before Enquiry of the Self. Enquiry of the mind needs to be conducted with honesty. Through honesty this step creates a strong foundation, increasing your capacity and eligibility to receive the truth that will result with Enquiry of the Self. When you become honest with yourself, you begin to understand the inner secrets, which the mind can never grasp. When the same honesty is used for Enquiry of the Self, you can achieve liberation from the cosmic illusion.

Q. 2 :   If we are not the mind, then why do we need to conduct enquiry of the mind?

Firstly, even though you are not the mind, yet from morning to night you are attached to the joys and sorrows created by the mind. By conducting its enquiry with honesty, your awareness will rise. With that, Enquiry of the Self will become easy for you.

Secondly, although you are not the mind, you are using the mind. Hence you should know about it. How much greed, ego, anger, hatred, malice, envy, lust, etc. it has. With all these patterns, in which direction is it going, how it gets entangled in the material world, and so forth.

Suppose you have gone shopping in the market. You are bargaining with the vendor but there is something else going on in your mind. Likewise watch yourself in every situation to check where you think one thing, speak something else, and act something totally different. With this investigation you will come to know whether there is harmony between your feelings, thoughts, words, and actions. Transformation will begin when such aspects come to light. Thereafter you will find that unnecessary stuff automatically drops off and only what is necessary will remain. This is the beauty of enquiry of the mind.

Before this enquiry, you used to feel there is someone standing in the dark and out of fear you wouldn't go there and hide under your covers. But now you are conducting enquiry and hence you go to see who it is. You discover that it is just a coat on a hanger. But if one concludes that whoever was there ran away, then is that correct? You know that the reality is nobody was there. This is what happens with the light of truth. You come to know that the separate individual ego due to which you indulged in greed, envy, etc. does not exist. This is the beauty of truth. When these aspects come to light, you will be liberated from the patterns of boredom, comparison, hatred, anger, etc. But for this to happen, you will have to observe your mind. Because the mind associates itself with the body and impacts the body, it is better to call enquiry of the mind as enquiry of the body-mind. Thus examine your body-mind from time to time and tell yourself honestly: "This is how my body-mind is. I have to function with this body-mind that I have received—however it may be."

Suppose you adopt a little child from an orphanage. As the child grows up and plays mischief, you say, "It's ok. However this child may be, I will raise it with love. This child has some tendencies of its biological parents but despite that I will care for it." In the same way, the tendencies of your body-mind have been inherited from your ancestors. Hence accept your body-mind as it is and work with it. But you should be aware of what all tendencies it has. When you will conduct enquiry of your body-mind with honesty, there is a possibility that these tendencies will start disappearing. If you don't enquire into them, they will stay. That is why it is essential to conduct this enquiry with honesty.

Q. 3 : Can we conduct this enquiry even when we have health problems?

Whenever you will look at your body-mind as separate from yourself, you will feel a sense of calm and peace. If you are entangled with the body-mind, you feel agitated. Do you feel troubled by standing before a hot mirror? You would say, "What difference does it make? Even if the mirror is hot, I can see myself in it." In the same way, even if your body-mind is sick or healthy, angry or peaceful, you can experience the Self through it. The only condition is that you should know what the Self is. If you don't have that knowledge, you will get attached to the body-mind and consider its suffering to be your suffering. Therefore you should conduct enquiry to know that the Self and the body-mind are two distinct entities.

Q. 4 : What exactly needs to happen in enquiry of the mind?

In this enquiry, you have to first start observing your mind in its different facets, in its different states, with different people, and in different relationships. You will discover how the mind changes from moment to moment, how it puts on various masks, how it compares, how it judges, how it forgets all its morals and principles when its ego is hurt, how it wants comforts and how it tries to escape from any discomfort, how it compromises on the truth for the sake of security, how it always thinks in the language of gain and loss, how it conjures up excuses and reasons, what all it does to get some praise, and so on.

Don't hide the reality from yourself. Report to yourself honestly without any deceit. You may not like to see your mind's darker aspects, but transformation will not occur without conducting an honest enquiry. If you really conduct enquiry of the body-mind with honesty, then this will become your foundation to attain Self realization.

Q. 5 : What has observation of the mind got to do with transformation?

Plenty. With correct observation, the wrong automatically ends. This is the beauty of awareness. You cannot get angry, kill somebody, or do something wrong in awareness. You can harm others only when you are unaware. You can be selfish only when you are unaware, since you are unable to feel the other person's pain. In this unawareness or unconsciousness, you cannot grasp the mysteries of life. Deceit, greed, ego, hatred, are all the offspring of unconsciousness. If you begin to watch yourself clearly in every situation, very soon you will be transformed. You will begin to understand the mind for the first time. The power of observation burns down the vices of the body-mind.

Q. 6 : Now I get it. So, how do I practice enquiry of the mind?

Every night just before going to sleep, if you look back at the entire day that has passed, or at least recall the major events of the day, then you will be able to understand the nature of your mind. Ask yourself, what were your actions in different situations and what was your underlying motive? If you did not do something that someone had asked you to, what was the reason? Was it because that person does not boost your ego? Or was it because they are a hurdle in the way of your ambitions and aspirations? On the other hand, if you did do something that you were asked to by someone, why did you do it? Was it because you were afraid of that person? Or was it because he or she boosts your ego? Do not hide from yourself. Answer honestly. If you like somebody, what is the reason? Is it because they do whatever you tell them to do or is it because of their qualities? If you do not like somebody, then are they really bad or is it just because they are an obstacle in your work? Answer in all seriousness.

After some days of this practice, you can then start observing your body-mind in every incident. Initially you may forget during some incidents. To develop the habit, there is a simple checklist that can help you. Check your mental state at an hourly interval throughout the day, against the following 12 points:

A – Anger. Feeling frustrated, irritated, or enraged on yourself or on others.

B – Boredom. Not feeling interested in anything.

C – Confusion. Not understanding in spite of explanations.

D – Depression. Feeling of melancholy even if there is no reason.

E – Ego. It is "I, me, myself…" Taking credit, self-praise.

F – Fear. Feeling scared, insecure, or uncertain.

G – Guilt. Self-criticism with the feeling, "Why did I do this?"

H – Happiness. Feeling good or joyous.

I – Ill-will. Hateful or malicious feeling, wanting to hurt someone.

J – Jealousy. Envy or feeling of "Why don't I have what others have?"

K – Kindness. Wanting to benefit or help others.

L – Laziness. Not wanting to do anything; being idle.

With such kind of observation at the end of every waking hour, you would come to know what your mental state is at that time. It is not important whether your state is good or bad, what's important is that you are prepared to look at yourself honestly.

Q. 7 : While conducting enquiry of the mind at an hourly interval or at any other time, suppose I find that my state is one of those listed against A-L, then how do I detach from that state?

You can detach from any state by understanding the secret of exactly what is happening to whom. In short: *Exactly what to whom?*

When you say, "I am bored," ask yourself at once, "Exactly who is getting bored? What is the meaning of bored? *I am getting bored* means exactly what is happening? And with whom is it happening?" You will then realize, "This is not happening with me, it is happening with the mind."

The conversation with yourself can be along the following lines:

- "What is happening?" The answer may arise, "I am getting bored."
- Then ask, "Who is getting bored? Me or the mind?" The answer will arise, "The mind is getting bored."
- You can then say, "If the mind is getting bored, let it. This is how the mind is."

In this way, by asking the right question at the right time, you can detach from the mind.

Q. 8 : Can you please explain this in further detail?

Suppose you are standing on the banks of a lake and your reflection is seen shaking on the surface of the water. If someone says, "Hey look, how you are shaking!" You would say, "That's my reflection, not me. If it's shaking, that doesn't mean I am shaking." In the same way, you should be clearly able to see that whatever is happening in your life is happening with whom. With this understanding, you cannot even imagine the transformation that will occur in your life.

Till date whenever the feeling of sorrow appeared, you said, "I am sad." Hereafter as soon as that feeling arises, ask the question: "Exactly who is sad?" A profound insight will emerge that it's never *you* who has felt the sorrow. *You* were always free, are free, and will always remain free. Because you were not aware of this, you always considered yourself to be the body-mind and said, "I am sad." But how can *you* be sad? Can you say, "This glass is filled with dry water"? No. Even a little child will say that either the glass must be filled with water or it must be dry. Both cannot exist together. Water cannot be dry, and if it dries, then it is not water anymore. Similarly, since your actual nature is happiness, then how can *you* be sad?

The one who is light itself, how can it become dark? When light disappears, only then people are able to perceive the existence of darkness. As long as there is light, darkness cannot exist. When you will enquire, "Exactly what to whom?", a lot will change inside you. Henceforth whenever any sorrow, boredom, hatred, lust, greed, or envy arises, ask, "Exactly what is happening? If anger has arisen, exactly what is happening? The body is trembling, heat is rising, the heart rate has increased, the face has become red, the eyes have become red…" Observe what is happening and to whom. When you will enquire with understanding, the answer that will come from within will be: "This is not happening with me. It is happening with this body-mind, which I am using."

Q. 9 : **If I observe my body-mind every day to see what it does, how would that benefit me? Rather, I may become unhappy thinking why I do whatever I do?**

You are not to become unhappy over issues like why you did something or why you did not do something. Understand that you are not conducting this enquiry to put yourself down, but to raise your level of awareness and realize the truth. You will see its benefits the next day. You will stop committing the same mistakes again and again. If you repeat the same behavior, something from within will alert you that very moment about what you are doing. You will rise above unconsciousness. Your awareness level will go up. It is this awareness that will later help you to discover who you really are.

If you feel dejected due to this enquiry, then you have missed the point; you are not enquiring correctly. Your mental disposition is due to the genes you have inherited from your parents, your upbringing, and your surroundings. These factors have made you what you are today. You are not the cause for your behavior. But after having become aware of your mind's behavior, if the same mistake is being repeated, then it's possible that you have not understood and applied this enquiry correctly. However, there is no need to be unhappy. All it means is that you have to work some more on your awareness. Whatever be your state today, accept yourself. Acceptance is miraculous. It is acceptance that takes you towards Bright happiness. Non-acceptance leads to unhappiness.

Q. 10 : What is Bright happiness?

Bright happiness or *Tej* happiness is the supreme bliss that is beyond joy and sorrow. It is causeless, constant, and is actually your true nature.

Q. 11 : Wow! How can I attain it? Can Self enquiry help in attaining it?

Yes, Enquiry of the Mind followed by Enquiry of the Self is one of the ways to attain it.

Q. 12 : Then I will definitely work on this method. I am also curious to know that, is fear, greed, or ego the reason behind all our actions? Is that why you are asking us to conduct enquiry of the mind?

When you think honestly, you will find that there are some expectations and some ego behind your every action. You have expectations from your parents, brother, sister, spouse, children, friends, and others. You want these expectations to be fulfilled. If they don't fulfill these expectations, they become the reason for your unhappiness and anger. In relationships, there should be *Tej* or Bright love and not just expectations. You should also not expect anything like name, fame, or gratitude for this love.

Q. 13 : What is Bright love? In fact, why do you use the word *Tej* or 'Bright'? What does it mean?

Many words that have traditionally been used in spirituality have gradually lost their true meaning with time and some words have even become corrupted. Hence a new term has been created which will help in understanding the essence of truth, which is *Tej* or Bright. It signifies the state which is absolute and is thus beyond duality, beyond polarity, beyond opposites. For instance, the opposite of success is failure. Similarly, hot and cold, up and down, love and hate are all pairs of opposites. But what is beyond both opposites is *Tej* or Bright. What is beyond love and hate is Bright love. What is beyond joy and sorrow is Bright happiness. There is no opposite to Bright happiness. It has no polarity because it is one. When you realize that *one*, you are liberated from duality, which is a construct of the mind. Here are some more examples:

Tejgyan / Bright Knowledge: The supreme wisdom which is beyond knowledge and ignorance.

Tej / Bright Truth: That which is beyond truth and falsehood. It signifies the supreme truth.

Tej / Bright Theist: The one who is beyond theism and atheism; the one who knows God alone exists.

Tej / Bright Friend: The one who is beyond friendship and enmity; the one who knows that everyone is one and the same.

Tej / Bright love: Love that is beyond love and hatred. It is unconditional and unquestioning love for one and all.

That's the kind of love we ultimately need to manifest. Bright love will emerge automatically through understanding of the truth. The ego will then dissolve.

Q. 14 : How is the ego created in the first place?

When we are 2-3 years old, the contrast mind begins to form, which then takes credit for every action that happens through the body. This is how ego is born and begins to grow. Different experiences, accomplishments, wealth, status, etc. further nourish and flourish the ego. Due to the habit of taking credit so as to get appreciation, we gradually become a slave to praise. There is no limit to the ego. One can never satisfy it; this is its nature. When we desire to feed the ego with praise and do not receive praise, we then have to bear its miseries as well. Enquiry of the mind and Enquiry of the Self will dissolve this ego and you will then discover your true essence. Most of your problems will end immediately. Enquiry is such a technique that if done with honesty and understanding can lead you to Self realization.

Q. 15 : If the contrast mind is the root of ego and all other problems, then how come we don't eradicate it as soon as it is formed?

That's because you don't recognize it for what it is, and hence continue to support it and make it stronger. A little story will drive home this point.

Once upon a time, there lived a couple in a village. One fine day, Uncle John visited their home. The husband was at work. Uncle John approached the wife and said, "I am Uncle John." The wife assumed that he must be her husband's uncle. Hence she welcomed him and made him comfortable. She served him food and then made a call to her husband to say that Uncle John has arrived. Her husband assumed that he may be her uncle. He said that he will return home soon. After reaching home, he met Uncle John and asked him, "How are you, Uncle John?" To which Uncle John replied that he is doing very well. With this, the wife was convinced that he was her husband's uncle. The husband continued to speak nicely to him assuming him to be his wife's uncle; he thought that if he did not speak properly to Uncle John, she may get upset thinking that he does not respect her relatives. At the same time, the wife also thought that she ought to treat Uncle John warmly as he was her husband's uncle. She asked Uncle John what he would like to have for dinner and he mentioned his choice based on his likes and dislikes.

In this way, Uncle John spent his remaining life in that house and one fine day he passed away. After his funeral when the couple returned home, the husband said, "Enough of pretence. Frankly speaking, had he not been your uncle, I would not have tolerated him even for a single day!" This is what happens when honesty is lacking. The wife was shocked. "My uncle!? I kept tolerating him only because he was your uncle!"

This story brings out the importance of enquiry. Had the couple enquired about his identity on the very first day of his arrival, Uncle John would have run away at once.

Uncle John is just a fictional name used here; do not hold any reference to anyone bearing the same name. Otherwise if somebody has an acquaintance called Uncle John, they may ask who he really is! Do not question others, question yourself.

Such an Uncle John (the contrast mind) resides within every human being, and as people never question it, it stays comfortably with them throughout their life. Every day it asks, "What are you going to feed me today? I like this, I do not like that..." You tend to fulfill all its desires but never doubt it. Under its influence you say, "Why did God do this? Why should we believe in God? Who is God?" But you never ask yourself, "Who *am* I? What is my purpose of coming to Earth?"

Q. 16 : What a brilliant analogy! Now I am beginning to understand. What else do I need to learn?

You have to learn a little and do a lot of unlearning. All beliefs and notions you have assumed and accepted have to be removed and cleared through understanding. Whosoever has the desire for love, joy, and peace should do this enquiry.

Q. 17 : So, we should initially begin enquiry of our body-mind just before going to sleep?

In the beginning, it is easy to do so just before retiring for the night. You will begin to understand your mind. For deeper enquiry, check yourself against A-L every hour of the day. (See Q6). Gradually, this enquiry will begin to happen immediately after any incident. As soon as any incident has occurred or any transaction has transpired, you will be able to see the emotions and desires hidden deep in your mind. You will be prepared to observe your ego. You will start seeing yourself, i.e. the ego, in various relationships. How you are different in front of your spouse as compared to in front of your household help. How you use deceit while shopping, or as a shopkeeper how you spin tales hiding something from your customer while highlighting something else. Later, you will become aware even before an incident. You will become aware of what you are about to do. There will be a transformation in your mind and thereby very soon this body-mind will become a medium to experience your true self.

Q. 18 : If this body-mind is a medium to experience my true self, how should I keep it pure?

Enquiry is a powerful method to purify the body-mind. As you practice it, the body-mind becomes progressively pure. This is because when you regularly conduct enquiry of the body-mind every day in every situation, very soon all the wrong tendencies, habits, and vices come to light. If your goal is to abide in the Self, then you will have to purify the body-mind so that it helps you in accessing and abiding in the Self.

Certain practices will help you in purifying the body. Firstly stop consuming junk food. Then ask yourself, "My body is the temple in which the Supreme Consciousness resides. So what should I introduce in this temple so that its purity increases?" This contemplation will raise your awareness and you will automatically stop eating too spicy or non-vegetarian food. This is because you will experience that such food increases lethargy and makes the body impure. Thereafter you will consume food only as required. You won't eat more or less than required by the body. Some people think they are vegetarians and hence their body is pure. But eating more food also makes the body heavy and lethargic, which is an invitation for diseases. Henceforth your choices should be based on the thinking that if you have to make your body a temple, then what you should put in it and what not. If you are able to do this, then it is divine devotion or divine love in the true sense. If devotion awakens within you, you would want to make your body a temple. You would not want any wrong habits or vices to remain in the body. Otherwise some people destroy their bodies with addictions such as drugs, drinking, smoking, gambling, etc. But due to devotion you would want to make your body addiction-free and pure. Then a new path will open up, that will lead you towards your ultimate goal.

Q. 19 : That's exactly what I want. So, if I want to enhance my understanding and fully benefit from enquiry of the mind, what should I do throughout the day?

During your waking hours, ask yourself a question at the end of every hour: "Right now, what is the state of my mind?" Check yourself against the 12 points from A to L. Then with the question, "Exactly what to whom?" detach from that state. With the hourly observation, you will get the insight that the desires of the mind and the state of the mind keep changing. Constant movement and change is its nature. Observe this mind. Sometimes you will find that the mind is anxious, sometimes happy, sometimes angry, sometimes full of greed, sometimes scared and withdrawn, and then sometimes worried or depressed. Sometimes it is full of hatred for somebody, and sometimes it is filled with guilt, sometimes egoistic and sometimes honest, sometimes deceitful, sometimes logical, sometimes comparing, sometimes imagining, sometimes unconscious, while sometimes fully aware. Enquiry of the mind every hour will have miraculous results. Very soon, you will know your mind completely.

By experience and not by mere intellect, you will know that the mind is just like a monkey that keeps jumping here and there. It cannot remain steady in any one state. *If that is how the mind is, then why do I get attached to it?!* This is the insight you will gain. Asking, "Exactly what to whom?" will make it clear that what you think is happening with you, is actually happening with the mind. *If the mind is disturbed, then it's not me who is disturbed.* This clarity will arise. This experience will influence your daily life. Thoughts of happiness or unhappiness will not be able to dislodge you from your centre. *It is the mind that is sad and it is the mind that is happy too. Anger, hatred, guilt, fear—all of these feelings are with the mind; not with me.* This understanding will dawn. *Changes in the mind every moment do not affect my Bright happiness in any way.* This is the wisdom that will emerge. You will then be peaceful from within even during stress. *Stress is with the body-mind, not with me. This stress has appeared to make the body perform a particular action.* Just as before examinations, a student experiences stress or fear, which makes him study. This will be the understanding you would have gained. As a result you will learn to witness with joy and peace everything that is happening with the body-mind.

You will know all the ups and downs at the experiential level and thus proceed towards Enquiry of the Self, which is the next step. At the first step, you carry out enquiry of the body-mind and observe its various behaviors in their entirety. At the second step, you come to know the one whose body-mind this is. Who is that? Who am I? Who was born? Who will die? Who sleeps? Who awakens? Who sits? Who walks? Who is it due to whose presence this entire universe is functioning? Who? Who?

• • •

*Returning to and abiding in your true nature
is the greatest devotion.
Cutting off thoughts as soon as they arise
by conducting Self enquiry
is true renunciation.*

3
ENQUIRY OF THE SELF

Q. 1 : After understanding and practicing enquiry of the mind, I am now eager to know about Enquiry of the Self. Please guide me further.

If you direct your attention to the place from where thoughts arise, you will realize your true self. The 'I' thought is the first thought. And that is why if you inquire, "Who am I?" continuously or devote some time every day to ask yourself this question in solitude, then the answer is bound to come. Answer, not from the intellect, but by actually being there. This question is the fundamental question or the first question that leads you towards the Self. Imagine that this 'I' thought has a body, then its 'feet' are rooted in the Self. Other thoughts arise from its 'head'. Till the 'I' thought does not arise, other thoughts do not arise. Go to the root or source of thoughts and the thoughtless state will manifest.

Q. 2 : How does the question "Who am I?" make the

mind thoughtless?

The mind is nothing but a bundle of thoughts. Being thoughtless means being in a 'no mind' state. To quiet the mind, 'Enquiry of the Self with understanding' is a very effective method. It will help you to make rapid progress on the spiritual path. When you ask "Who am I?", which is also a thought in the form of a question, it will cut off other thoughts, it will end all other thoughts. While this enquiry is being conducted, other thoughts cannot form.

When you close your eyes and watch your thoughts, right behind the thoughts is the Self. The train of thoughts goes on. To reach the Self, you join a thought of your own, which is the question of Self enquiry. Imagine there is a train passing by. You are watching it and the train seems to go on and on, with so many bogies one after the other—it's endless. However, if you were to add a bogie of your own, the train finally ends. Similarly, to the unending train of thoughts, the bogie that you have to attach is the question: "Who am I?" This is your true self's thought. Learn to add this thought from your side. When you sit with eyes closed in meditation and thoughts seem to emerge one after the other, you should say, "Fine, let me add a bogie of my own." With this addition, the length of the train of thoughts reduces. As soon as you feel there are many thoughts crowding the mind, ask, "Who am I?" and see what happens. After ending all other thoughts, this last thought of 'Who am I?' will also end itself. You will be left with nothing, but pure consciousness. That's the Self. Experiencing it is Self realization. You will realize that you are separate from the body. You are not limited to the body. You are boundless and boundaryless. You will realize this at the experiential level.

Q. 3 : So, I should start asking the question, "Who am I?" and then I will know who I am?

To know who you are, first ask yourself, "Who I am not?" You have already ruled out that you are not the mind by conducting enquiry of the mind. Now rule out everything else that you are not and then you will know who you are. A small story will help in understanding this point.

A woman was ill. She had a dream in which she was standing at the gates of heaven and calling out, "Let me in." From inside the gates came a voice: "Who are you?" She replied, "I am a politician's wife." The voice said, "Who asked you about your husband? Tell me who you are." She thought about it and said, "I am the mother of four children." The voice boomed again, "Who asked you about your children? Simply state who you are." She hesitatingly answered, "I am a teacher." The voice said, "Who asked you about your profession? Why don't you answer, who are you?" Unsure about what is being asked, she said, "I am a Christian." The voice said, "Nobody asked you about your religion or caste. Who are you?" She could not give the right answer till the end, and out of fear, she woke up and her eyes opened. After her eyes opened, her life transformed.

When you look at a bicycle, exactly what do you call as the bicycle? Are the wheels the bicycle? No. Are the handles the bicycle? No. Are the pedals the bicycle? No. Is the seat the bicycle? No. Then what is the bicycle? 'Bicycle' is just a word that has been given for convenience. In the same way, 'I' is also a thought given for convenience. You have to enquire about this 'I'.

Thus, first contemplate, "Who I am not?"

- I am not this body because the moment I say this is "*my* body," it is something outside of me. It is not me. I am not *my* car. *My* house cannot be me. Thus, *my* body cannot be me.
- The name given to this body is not me.
- The five elements of this physical body, i.e. earth, fire, water, air, and ether, are not me.
- My astral body is not me.
- The five sense organs of the body, i.e. eyes, ears, nose, tongue, and skin, are not me.
- I am not the five senses—sight, sound, smell, taste, and touch.
- I am also not the breath due to which this body-mind functions.
- I am not the mind that thinks about what I should be.
- I am not the intellect that is absent along with the body during deep sleep.

Q. 4 :   If I am none of the above, then who am I?

You are the one that remains. It is you who uses the physical and the astral body. It is you who is the master of the intellect and the senses. It is you who is the witness of the mind. You are beyond every label. And if you are not the body, mind, or intellect…

- how can you be an engineer or a doctor or a leader or a student?
- how can you be a brother or a sister, a father, a mother, a husband, a wife, a friend, a son, a daughter, a disciple, or a Guru?
- how can you be American, Indian, British, or Italian?
- how can you be a Hindu, a Muslim, a Christian, or a Jew?
- how can you be white, black, brown, or yellow?
- how can you be thin, fat, tall, short, beautiful, or ugly?
- how can you be cheerful, intelligent, foolish, positive, honest, pious, active, or lazy?

Now it is just you who remains—pure, stateless, without any name or form. Accept your true nature as it is. And remain that. You have become something that you are not due to the belief that you are the body. Now it is time to get established in Consciousness, to be who you really are and abide in it.

Q.5: What happens when we ask, "Who am I?"

As soon as you ask the question "Who am I?" you come out of unconsciousness and become aware to receive the answer. This question pierces you like an arrow and drives you within to your centre. In the beginning you may not be able to recognize the deep silence or stillness within you in spite of reaching your centre (the Source or Self). However, by persisting with this question, you will gradually begin to recognize that state of consciousness which is your true self.

Thoughts are always running in the mind. You need a very powerful thought to annihilate these thoughts—a thought that will annihilate all other thoughts. You need steel to cut steel. An antidote for a poison is poison. In the same way, let one thought annihilate all other thoughts. 'Who am I?' is a thought that will end every thought, notion, belief, and concept. All you need is to learn how to use this powerful weapon.

Q. 6 : How should I practice 'Enquiry of the Self with understanding'?

This is how 'Enquiry of the Self with understanding' is practiced: Whenever a thought appears, be it of fear, greed, hatred, worry, frustration, depression, or anything else, ask yourself, "To whom has this thought occurred?" Or ask, "Who was afraid?" Or, "Who felt depressed?" The answer will arise, "I." Now ask, "Who is this 'I'? Who am I?" Attempt to locate this 'I'. Keep your attention in the area of your heart. Do not worry about being successful in locating it. By attempting to locate the 'I', your mind will drop and you will reach the state of inner silence for some time. Another thought will appear after a few moments. You will again ask the question, "To whom has this thought occurred?" The reply will be, "To me." Ask again, "Who is this *me*? Who am I?" Again, attempt to locate this 'I'. In the process, the mind shall again drop. What will remain will be just your true self, the Self, the Consciousness, the experience of *being*, the stillness, the infinity. Thus, the answer to "Who am I?" is the state it leads to. This is the understanding that is most important in the practice of Enquiry of the Self with understanding.

You may begin by performing this enquiry every day for 20 minutes. You will close your eyes and sit in a comfortable posture, where the spine is straight but not tensed. Try to keep your body completely still. Let your breathing continue normally. Then begin the process of Enquiry of the Self. It's better to practice it right at the beginning of the day, so that you can enter your daily life as the real you. Very soon you will be able to conduct this enquiry even while working or carrying out your everyday activities, with eyes open, of course.

Q. 7 : While practicing Enquiry of the Self, how should we answer the question "Who am I?"

It is very important to understand this. A seeker asks himself, "Who am I?", and then proceeds to answer it intellectually, "I am this" or "I am not this." However, the idea behind 'Enquiry of the Self with understanding' is that you are not supposed to give the answer merely in words, but instead you have to go to the source of thoughts. You have to go to that feeling at your centre. By attempting to locate the 'I', you have to let the mind drop so that you are in a no-mind state, even if it is just for a few seconds. This way, by constant practice, you will start *being* on yourself, and eventually the whole day long the mind itself would like to go back to your centre or source. The internal feeling is important, not the answer by the intellect. You have to drop into the place from where thoughts originate.

Q. 8 : Where is that place? Where is the centre or

source? Different authors or teachers describe the centre at different locations on the body. Kindly clarify this issue.

We call the centre or source as the *tejasthan*. Tejasthan literally means the Bright Place. It is the place where the Self connects with the body; where the formless and the form unite; where the union takes place. It can be roughly considered to be in the area of the heart. It is not a single point, but can be taken as the entire area of the heart.

Q. 9 : Thank you for clarifying that. So, during Enquiry of the Self, we have to repeatedly ask, "Who am I?"

One might commit the mistake of continuously asking, "Who am I? Who am I? Who am I?" without pausing for the answer to emerge or without ever *being* on the sense of *being*. With this kind of mechanical repetition, Enquiry of the Self is converted into just another mantra. It may reap the benefit of mechanical repetition of a mantra, but will not lead to Self realization. On the other hand, by asking "Who am I?" even once, if you are experiencing your true self or sense of *being*, then it is enough. After asking this question, attempt to locate the 'I' and keep your entire attention focused at your centre, on the sense of *being*. Stay in that experience as long as possible until the next thought appears.

In the early days of your practice, you will have to ask the question "Who am I?" several times because the mind's tendency is to stray. You will have to ask the question repeatedly to bring it back to the source. Initially there will be more unconsciousness and less consciousness. With regular practice, the mind will begin to stay at the source by merely asking the question once or twice. Consciousness will rise, unconsciousness will reduce, due to which Self enquiry will become easier.

Q. 10 : Suppose a thought arises. When should we ask, "To whom is this thought occurring?"

Some might assume that when a thought arises, only after completely thinking over that thought, they should ask themselves as to whom is this thought occurring. No. As soon as you become aware of a thought emerging, cut it off at that very moment by asking, "To whom is this thought occurring? From where is this thought arising? If it is occurring to me, then who am I?" Focus on your centre and remain in the experience of *being*. With daily practice for some time, this will become easy.

Q. 11 : How can we continuously conduct this enquiry? It is natural for thoughts to arise constantly. In such situations, how can we reach the Self?

If understood correctly, this enquiry is not difficult at all. It does not matter how many thoughts appear. As soon as a thought arises, simply ask the questions mentioned earlier. You will be thrown back to yourself. Remember, do not give the answer merely in words. Do not answer from the intellect saying, "I am Consciousness... I am the Self..." etc. What is more important is to attempt to locate the 'I'. If possible, you can close your eyes and carry out this process.

Dropping the mind and reaching the experience of the Self is the real answer to this question.

By conducting Enquiry of the Self in this manner, every thought will take you back every time to your true self. Right now, if you are thinking, "I am not able to understand this," then ask, "Who is it that is unable to understand? If 'I' cannot understand, then who is this 'I'... who... who...?" Immediately you will find that thoughts disappear for a few moments. You become thoughtless. Only the Self remains. In this way, by repeatedly going onto the Self, the mind will weaken and the Self present behind it will begin to shine. By repeated practice, the mind will learn to stay at its source. By dipping into the Self again and again, the mind will dissolve. It is like the story of the dolls made of salt. They wanted to dive into the sea to measure its depth. But slowly, they themselves dissolved.

Q. 12 : Ultimately what happens with Enquiry of the Self?

With deep Enquiry of the Self when only your *being* remains, then the question "Who am I?" also dissolves. Such a deep silence will manifest that the one who asks "Who am I?" will no longer be there. For the first time you will know that true happiness is only in absolute silence. The questioner shall vanish with the mind. After all, a question is but a part of the mind. Answers in words also belong to the mind. Both shall merge in the source of thoughts that has manifested. Then, only the truth remains.

Q. 13 : How long should we practice Enquiry of the Self?

Enquiry of the Self should be practiced till you fully recognize and realize your true essence. Till your root belief 'I am the body' breaks. The evidence of your successful practice of 'Enquiry of the Self with understanding' will be that all the wrong beliefs and notions about yourself are shattered. Thereafter Enquiry of the Self will stop because you will then be stabilized in your true self. Thereafter when thoughts arise, you would know: *These thoughts are not mine, nor do they occur to me. I am beyond everything. I am simply the seer or the Bright witness*. Thoughts are occurring in this body-mind. This body-mind is my mirror. If thoughts are running in my mirror, why should I have a problem? The mirror shows my true self to me and helps me to experience it.*

Returning to and abiding in your true nature is the greatest devotion. Cutting off thoughts as soon as they arise by conducting Enquiry of the Self is true renunciation or detachment.

Q. 14: Should we first clear all our doubts and then begin this practice?

Read the guidelines given in the next chapter. In fact, read this book repeatedly so as to understand the technique clearly. Then begin the enquiry with whatever understanding you reach at that point of time. With repeated enquiry, you will begin to understand the rest.

• • •

---

*Bright Witness: Bright witnessing means 'seeing as it is' or seeing the reality. This is distinct from the witnessing by the mind. The Bright Witness is the Self which also witnesses the mind's witnessing.

With Self Enquiry,
your problems are not solved, they dissolve.
You won't get rid of the disease, but of the patient itself.
You won't get happiness, but will become happiness itself.

4
GUIDELINES FOR SELF ENQUIRY

Q. 1 :   What are the guidelines for Self enquiry?

Firstly begin with self-acceptance. Accept your body-mind as it is, including your face, height, weight, intelligence level, mental and social behavior and skills. We often accept only a part of life, resulting in unhappiness. We accept joy, but not sorrow. Success is acceptable, but failure is not. We accept respect, but not disrespect. The right hand is acceptable, while the left is considered lowly by some communities. Some of us accept the upper part of our body, but not the lower. Some of us accept our body externally, but not internally. Part acceptance means conflict. Conflict always leads to sorrow. Hence accept yourself fully, stop constricting yourself with non-acceptance, and start living openly. Everything, including spiritual practice, will then be easier.

Q. 2 : Are we always supposed to practice Self enquiry in a seated position with eyes closed?

No. In the beginning it helps to practice Self enquiry in a sitting position with eyes closed. Practicing in the morning for at least 20 minutes is essential. But later on, besides this morning practice, the enquiry can continue when you are walking, working, or carrying out all your day-to-day activities. You will reach the source many times throughout the day. Remembrance of your true self will increase. "Who became sad?" "Who became happy?" "Who got upset?" Every question will take you back to the Self, because you have to answer not merely in words, but attempt to locate the 'I'. In the process the mind will drop and you will reach the Self. In fact, you move away from the Self because of thoughts and words. This practice takes you back to the Self.

Q. 3 : What are the guidelines regarding posture, time, periodicity, breathing, etc. during Self enquiry?

Self enquiry can be practiced at any time, any place, and in any posture. Initially it helps to practice at a fixed time and place, in the seated position. You can always use a *mudra* (a special way of holding your fingers) too. All of these are helpful, especially in the beginning, but not essential. What is more important is that Self enquiry should be practiced regularly and consistently. There should not be even a day's break, which can become the cause for laziness. Just like we have meals at least twice a day, practice Self enquiry at least once or twice a day. As your consistency increases, Self enquiry will become second nature to you—just like breathing. This is possible with consistent practice.

In the beginning, practice with eyes closed until you have mastered the practice. With eyes open, there is a possibility of the mind going astray after external objects. Your breathing should be normal while practicing Self enquiry. There is no need to regulate it.

For being consistent, you can consider practicing Self enquiry in a group. While practicing in a group if someone begins to avoid the practice, then others can encourage and inspire them, remind and motivate them to practice. A group can prove to be inspirational because the aim of all members is the same.

Q. 4 :   Any other essential instructions?

Other essential instructions are:

1) Do not be in a hurry while beginning the Self enquiry session. Carry out all the activities before the session such as taking a bath, arranging a seat, etc. with patience. Every activity should be carried out in a slow and calm manner with a feeling of surrender. There is no need for impatience and haste.

2) It is more helpful if you have a spiritual master or a teacher because then you can share your experiences of the enquiry with him/her and receive guidance. If you don't have a master or teacher, then without paying attention to the physical or mental experiences during

Self enquiry, you should continue practicing it regularly.

3) There should be no hurry even after completing Self enquiry. Let the body get up and start walking in a normal manner at normal speed. Do not try to hurry from your side. Allow the experience of *being* to continue as long as possible.

Q. 5 : What is the difference between Enquiry of the Mind and Enquiry of the Self?

In enquiry of the mind, you watch the mind and its workings. You get the insight that the mind is constantly changing and you are not the mind. That's why enquiry of the mind helps you to detach from the mind, detach from the thoughts. On the other hand, in enquiry of the Self, you attempt to reach the very source of thoughts. You go beyond the mind to the real you. But carrying out enquiry of the mind at the first step helps because then during Self enquiry you can easily push the mind aside and go beyond it since you already know that the real you is not the mind. You can go deeper to discover the Self.

Q. 6 : What is the relationship between Self enquiry and inner silence (*moun*)?

The reality is that your true nature is Absolute Silence or stillness. You are not to become silent; you simply have to know that you are Silence. You are in fact *Tej* or Bright Silence, which is the state beyond sound and silence, beyond speech and thought. Words appear from this inner silence and also disappear in it. There is silence between every word and behind every word. There is silence between every thought and behind every thought. On the paper of silence, the words of thought are written. To attain this silence is to attain the Self. It is attachment to thoughts that causes sorrow. By conducting Self enquiry, you go beyond the body, mind, and intellect, and reach the Bright Silence within. That's the Self.

Q. 7 : Sometimes while practicing Self enquiry, I reach my centre but there is nothing within; I can't see the Self.

One may say that when there are no thoughts, there is nothing within. One says this because we are habituated to only imagine something confined to form and shape. Hence we are unable to imagine ourselves formless and shapeless. We cannot believe that we can exist without the body. We are the formless Self. When we are the Self, how will we see the Self? Who shall remain to see the Self separately? Rather, there will just be the experience of *being*. The experience (Self) experiences the experience (Self) in the experience (Self). The mind does not experience this; this experience does not occur to the mind. But the mind would repeatedly like to come and have a look at it.

When in deep sleep, who wants to come and have a look whether you are actually asleep or not? It is only when you wake up in the morning that you know you had slept. It is the mind (thoughts) that goes to sleep and the mind that awakens. There is no question of believing or not believing that you were in deep sleep. Do you require a mirror to know yourself? Even without a mirror, you know that you *are*. There is no need for any proof.

Q. 8 : Sometimes during Self enquiry, I see lights or colors. What should I do at that time?

During Self enquiry, you may experience various phenomena such as the sense of being bodyless, hearing sounds or music, seeing light or various colors, or stars and space, and so forth. Such experiences belong to the realm of the mind. You have to enquire who is it that is seeing this light? Who is it that is listening to this sound? And thus you reach the real Witness, the Self.

Q. 9 : My mind does not support me and I can hardly stay in the experience of Self; if at all.

In the beginning, being on your Self will occur for short periods of time. But further on, it will become natural and simple—you can even walk and talk while being on your true self. That is what has been termed as *Sahaj Samadhi* or Effortless Samadhi. Until you experience your *beingness* or the bliss within, your mind will resist surrendering to the experience. But once it gets the taste, it would want to dissolve in that experience repeatedly. Hence continue with the Self enquiry.

Samadhi, as you may know, is the state of consciousness before time began. It is a state which cannot be adequately expressed in words; it can only be experienced. It can be said that Samadhi is being one with the true self, transcending time and space. Or being in the state of undifferentiated beingness; a state of complete peace and joy.

Q. 10 : When I am unable to feel the experience of *being*, I feel upset.

During a practice session, when you feel that you are unable to reach the experience of *being*, the mind gets upset and desires to have that experience. It wants to have the same experiences that occurred during the previous session. Due to this ignorance, it begins to enquire in the wrong direction. Do not fight with the mind. Actually it is the mind that wants to fight the mind. So instead of fighting the mind, you should simply look at it as a witness and ask, from where do all these thoughts originate? Go to your centre and experience your *being*.

Q. 11 : What are the wrong notions about Self enquiry?

Some might think that this is just a technique for suppressing thoughts or for improving concentration. It is not so. The purpose of this technique is to reach your source or centre. Improvement in concentration occurs automatically with Self enquiry as a byproduct. This practice does not suppress thoughts, instead by this technique thoughts dissolve into the eternal silence (*moun*) within. This silence itself is the eternal bliss.

Q. 12 : What are the pitfalls in the process of Self

enquiry?

Impatience is a major pitfall. The mind desires the fruit of labor immediately. "Today I did Self enquiry. So how did I benefit?" This is what the mind wants to check. If it does not find any benefit, it tends to stop the enquiry. It loses patience in the desire for some benefit. However, the fact is that you are carrying out your spiritual practice to get freedom from loss and gain. Therefore, do not expect the fruit of this practice. Simply continue with the enquiry every day, every hour, and every situation, with patience, and you will definitely receive the fruit. Also understand that impatience is just another facet of the mind. Enquire, "Who is impatient?"

Your mind may repeatedly bring up the thought: "How much longer should I continue with Self enquiry?!" Do not entertain any such doubts. Otherwise the mind will lead you astray. Continue this practice with faith. Very soon you will see the miracles it brings forth.

Q. 13 : I feel that Self enquiry is a difficult practice because it requires a lot of willpower, time, and patience.

Do not automatically assume that Self enquiry is a difficult practice and it is something that requires great willpower, patience, and time. This is a wrong and baseless assumption. The reality is that if you develop the understanding that the treasure house of bliss is the silence within, then the mind itself would like to go there. The mind is like a bee that hops from one flower to another. When it finds a flower with honey, it becomes still and stays there. When the mind finds true happiness within, it stops wandering outside. As a result, your strength, willpower, and patience increase automatically.

Q. 14 : If I reach my true self, then will all my problems be solved?

The moment you enquire who is it to whom these problems occur, you will realize that problems are with the body-mind. You consider yourself as the body-mind and thus assume that those problems are your problems and suffer from them. With Self enquiry, problems are not solved, they dissolve. You won't get rid of the disease, but of the patient itself. You won't get happiness, but will become happiness itself. Additionally, the energy that is usually spent in thoughts is conserved, due to which your work capacity and creativity also increase.

Q. 15 : How can I be happy? How can Self enquiry help me with that?

As long as we need a reason to be happy, we can never be happy. This is because the reason might be there today, but may not be present tomorrow. The happiness you experience without any reason is Bright happiness. It is beyond joy and sorrow. Such causeless happiness is experienced only due to your *being*. This happiness is neither due to gaining something nor losing something. This happiness does not diminish with time. It is unbroken and boundless bliss. Self enquiry will help you to achieve it.

If you get the knack of Self enquiry, you will automatically learn the art of constantly *being* on your true self, which is eternal happiness. This will take some effort at first, but later on it will happen easily. It is quite possible that it may take some time to develop this knack, but when you do, then this time invested will become the best investment of your life.

But be patient. Do not be in a hurry. The notion that I should get quick results (results that the mind likes or the results as defined by the ideas of the mind) is an obstacle to proper enquiry. Impatience makes the mind restless. Try to make it cool and calm because the sun of understanding does not rise easily in a mind filled with thoughts. By ending the thoughts with enquiry, the sun of understanding will rise in all its glory.

Q. 16 : How is Self enquiry different from other meditation techniques?

Self enquiry is a two-in-one technique. When you begin to doubt the individual (personal I, individual ego, sense of separateness), only then does the individual begin to disappear. Otherwise it continues to live like a patient. For example, you may have seen pictures of Mother India in the form of a goddess. But if you say you want to actually see that goddess, you will be told there is no such goddess. Such images have been created for children to make them understand the concept of a country and to awaken the feelings of patriotism. This is because children understand better through the medium of stories and pictures. In the same way, through Self enquiry you will understand that the individual does not exist. It is just an image which has been created by the formless Self to experience itself.

As soon as you begin Self enquiry, you will find it miraculous that it's so easy to understand the supreme truth. Just by conducting Self enquiry, you begin to understand it. That's because the truth that you are seeking is already available and it is within you. You don't have to attain it from outside. When you start practicing Self enquiry, the false 'I', which considers itself to be a separate individual, begins to disappear. It is due to this sense of separateness and of being limited that you feel anxious, hopeless, or helpless. Hence whenever you feel any negative emotion, ask yourself at once, "Who is anxious? Who is helpless?" When you will go inside and see, you will find no one, just blankness. If some moments later again the thought appears, "I am anxious," then again ask, "Who is anxious?"

When you decide to practice Self enquiry daily, you will find that the first day you will remember to practice it only for a short time. Later on the duration of remembrance will go on increasing. Gradually all the events occurring around you will become an opportunity for Self enquiry. If you feel hungry, you will say, "Who is feeling hungry?" You can ask the question for everything.

Nowadays the aim behind the spiritual practices or meditation techniques that most people practice is to increase concentration. They may sit for half an hour and observe their breath. This definitely increases their concentration but they are unable to reach the experience of Self. On the other hand, Self enquiry results in double benefit. Firstly, your concentration increases because the mind repeatedly goes within and begins to become quiet and stable. Secondly, you attain the experience of Self.

Q. 17 : Oh! I now understand the beauty of Self enquiry. But I was wondering, are there no other ways to quiet the mind?

Making the mind quiet is just one of the steps in Self enquiry. It is not the goal. If after silencing the mind, the understanding of truth does not arise, then you are not using Self enquiry as you ought to. You may be using it mechanically like any other mantra or technique. If you practice Self enquiry with understanding, then you realize and experience the truth. Understanding of truth does not arise with other techniques. Some people try to quiet the mind by regulating their breath (*pranayama*) or chanting a *mantra*. With these methods, one does feel that the mind has become quiet for some time. However, due to lack of understanding of truth, the mind returns after some time with its same old understanding and doubts. Thoughts continue to trouble them. When one focuses the mind in the gap between two breaths, then too the mind becomes quiet. One begins to feel that along with breathing, the mind too has stilled. But in deep sleep, even while the breath continues, the mind is quiet or even ceases to exist. But that does not change one's understanding. Self enquiry achieves silencing of the mind naturally in addition to realizing the true self.

Q. 18 : Do we attain both wisdom and devotion with Self enquiry?

Yes. So far you have learned 'Self enquiry with understanding' which helps you attain wisdom experientially. As it is said, the difference between knowledge and wisdom is 'experience'. With the practice of Self enquiry, you will realize your true nature and gain the insight that the Self that is experienced is the same in each and everyone—it is the Universal Self.

Self enquiry when practiced consistently will also help in frequent remembrance of the Self, which is what devotion is all about. Many seekers practice Self enquiry for a few days and then stop practicing it. That is why the method of 'Enquiry in the Now' has been introduced in the next chapter, which makes Self enquiry more easy and practical. This will help you immensely in remembering the Self throughout the day and thus enhance your level of devotion.

● ● ●

God lives in the space of present,
and when you too are in the present,
then you are with God,
you are God.

5
ENQUIRY IN THE NOW

Q. 1: I am getting a glimpse of my true nature through Self enquiry. But the problem is that I face various situations during my everyday activities, due to which I get caught up in anger, fear, worry, hatred, etc. At that time, it is difficult to shift to my true self. What should I do at such times?

Let us look at a story to understand what you can do at such times.

A man was desperately searching for a job, but had no success despite his best efforts. He was struggling a lot, and then he suddenly remembered a friend who was working abroad. He called his friend, and explaining his situation, requested for help in finding a job. His friend immediately invited him over and promised him a good job. The man was overjoyed, but also felt a bit anxious. He asked, "I have no experience in working overseas, so will I be getting some training for the job?" His friend assured him that he would certainly receive the required training. The man was pleased and asked him where they would meet. His friend gave him the address of a hotel and asked to meet him at 10 o' clock on a particular date at a gala function being organized on the grounds of the hotel.

The man had one more question. He said, "I don't understand the language that is spoken in your country. If I don't see you when I reach there, what should I do, since I would neither be able to ask or answer anything if someone were to speak to me?" The friend told him, "Don't worry. On reaching there, if you face any problem in dealing with someone, or if someone asks you something that you cannot understand, just say, 'WAIN'. When you say WAIN, your problem will be solved and no one will bother you." The man, though surprised, was happy to hear this and readily agreed to do it.

As decided, the man took a plane and reached the meeting place on the given date. Due to the time difference between the two countries, he reached at 10 a.m., whereas his friend had asked to meet him at 10 p.m. The man did not remember this and started searching for his friend in the grand function that was underway on the grounds of the hotel. He could not find him and that's when he realized that his friend had set the meeting at 10 p.m. according to the time in this country. Now he was in a dilemma as to how he would spend the whole day! Just then the concierge at the hotel approached him and said, "Sir, why are you standing here? You are blocking the flow of the guests walking in." The man could not understand the language and hence did not know what was said to him. He immediately recalled what his friend had told him to do when faced with any problem, and he said, "WAIN." The concierge said, "Okay," and went away. The man was relieved.

Now he started wandering around, checking out the arrangements and the food stalls. A waiter walked up to him and told him something in the native language. Again our man did not understand anything and hence once again he said, "WAIN." Amazingly, the waiter went away at once.

It was like a carnival going on with a lot of entertainment and food and drinks. The man enjoyed everything, and whenever he had a problem or confusion in dealing with anyone, he said, "WAIN." With this word, no one said anything and the situation got sorted out. This went on for the whole day.

Finally, when his friend arrived, he found this man playing with some children. He had made friends with the kids and was having fun with them. When our man saw his friend, he rushed towards him and hugged him with joy. He also explained that he had mistakenly arrived at ten in the morning. They both had a good laugh and then his friend took him to his suite in the hotel and ordered dinner. They enjoyed their food while catching up with each other. As it was late, they decided to retire for the night and talk about the job the next morning.

On waking up the next morning, the friend could not find the man in his room. He started searching for him and came down and found him busy helping the hotel staff as well as speaking to the guests of the hotel. The friend was surprised to find him adjusting so quickly in the new place and mingling with all the people around. The friend approached the man and told him, "Looks like you are already settled here." He replied, "I am enjoying this place a lot. Now tell me about my job and what kind of training do I need?" The friend laughed and said, "You are already on the job and you are trained as well. I had called you to work as a manager in this hotel and you are already doing that job very well. There is no need of any interview, you are selected, and the job is yours."

Q. 2 : **That's an interesting story! But what does 'WAIN' mean? And how will it help me in returning to my true nature when I am caught up in anger, fear, etc.?**

We will see how this story will help you by understanding the meaning of this story and the meaning of WAIN as well.

The man in the story was quite anxious in the beginning; but what training did he receive throughout the day? The answer is 'WAIN.' It stands for "Who am I *now*?" We will call it as Enquiry in the Now.

The problems that occurred with the man in the story are common occurrences in our daily lives too. We do not fully understand the behaviors and intent and communication (analogous to language in the story) of the people interacting with us, and think:

- Why do these people behave in such a rude manner?
- Why is that person looking angrily at me?
- Why don't my colleagues respect me?
- Why don't my friends help me?
- Why doesn't my spouse listen to me?
- Why doesn't the office boy obey me?
- Why does my neighbor use such words with me?
- Why does my boss think I am worthless? Does this mean I don't do my job well?
- If I praise someone (even though it may be false praise), he/she immediately starts respecting me.

An average person often faces such situations in life. Reflect upon your life and see which situations upset you. In the story, when the man's friend had not arrived at the appointed place, how upsetting it would have been. If he did not have the word 'WAIN' to help him, how unhappy he would have been. How difficult it would have been to wait from morning till night. He may have possibly run away.

With the wisdom of "Who am I now?", life becomes easy. We always think, "If this happens, then I will be happy... If that happens, then I will be happy... I will be happy when I retire... I will be happy if I have this much money... Let me settle down, let me get this house, this car, get married... then I will be happy." But actually what happens? One flees from every problem and keeps waiting for the next scene to be happy. As a result, one gets stuck in the web of the past and the future. The 'Who Am I Now?' (WAIN) mantra anchors you in the present and helps Consciousness to shine.

Q. 3 : Why "Who am I now?" I have never heard of it before.

Good question. Let's understand this. "Who am I?" is the question that is traditionally asked in the practice of Self enquiry. Self enquiry is an ancient method of Self realization, which has been revived once more in the recent past. However, its finer nuances have gone missing again and it has become one of the most misunderstood of subjects. The understanding behind the method, the finer nuances, and the missing links have been explained to you previously so that you can practice Self enquiry in the best manner and gain the most from it.

But why "Who am I now?" Well, in the modern times, there are so many activities and so many distractions at any given moment that people get deeply entangled in them. They are unable to detach themselves from the physical and mental world, so as to remember who they are. Hence a modern version is needed for busy people, so that Self enquiry can be easily practiced not only every day but several times a day. "Who am I now?" helps you to instantly drop your assumed personality and the mind and come out of its entanglements. You have never heard about it before because it did not exist before. "Who am I?" is a sort of immersive experience, while "Who am I now?" is an immediate experience.

Now what happens with the one who has the wisdom of "Who am I now?" In the story you saw the man playing with kids and enjoying himself. It's a new place, a new environment, new people, new language, new culture, everything is different, yet he is happy. What is the secret that he knows? You need to know the same secret—the art of being in the present. Whenever you are in any problematic situation, ask yourself, "WAIN" or "Who am I now?" The mind will drop and you will shift to the present moment. Being in the present itself is a state of supreme bliss.

With this understanding try an experiment. During any problem, situation, or state, first ask yourself, "Who was I a moment back?" The answer could be: "A moment back I was...

- an arrogant person
- an upset person
- a scared person

- a bored person
- a confused personality
- an angry or irritable person
- someone who was calm and peaceful
- an intelligent or smart person
- a loser or a doormat
- someone who was comparing myself with others…

But, "Who am I now?" Ask yourself, "A moment back I was so and so, but who am I now?" As soon as you say, "Who am I now?" you will be pulled back from your mental web and from your personality into the present moment and be reminded of your true self. You will attempt to locate the real 'I' just like in Enquiry of the Self, and be led back to the experience of *being*. You will then find that the problem or situation has dissolved.

In the story, what did that man do from 10 o'clock in the morning till 10 o'clock at night? He was actually practicing WAIN. Because in every situation, whether he was confused or anxious, he was continuously saying WAIN or "Who am I now?" If you do the same, you can constantly stay in the experience of Self.

Suppose you get a thought, "Oh! I don't look good. This dress doesn't suit me." Immediately ask, "Who am I now?" You will shift to the present, remember who you actually are, and then go to the experience of Self. If you get the thought, "Why am I so short?" Say, "Who am I now?" Your thoughts will change and you will say, "So what if this body is short? The real me is taller and bigger than this entire universe." In this way, by associating any thought with "Who am I now?" you can shift to the present moment and thereby to your real self.

Q. 4 : All spiritual masters emphasize on being in the present. Why is the present so important?

The present is not time, it is space. On the scale of time, we say the moment between the past and the future is the present. But that is not the present, that's a window through which you enter and pass behind the scale of time. Time ends there and behind is the vast space. That is the present. The present is where time and space become one. The feeling is that of timelessness and that space is divine space.

Where does God* (Self or Consciousness) live? What is the address of God? In what time does God live? God does not live in time, God lives in space. You too live in space, but God does not live in that space. When you go to the space that God lives in, that is called the present. God lives in the space of present, and when you too are in the present, then you are with God, you are God. Because there is no one there to check: *Am I God? I should check how come I am*

---

*You can read Enquiry about God and *Beliefs* in Appendix-I of this book.

God? The one who is asking these questions is the individual ego—the sense of separateness from God. This ego is so small. But you know that even if a little something gets in your eye, you are unable to see a huge mountain. Likewise, this little sense of separateness, that you identify with, does not allow you to see the infinite Self—which is your true nature. This little speck of ego shrouds the infinite God. But even this is a game of God himself.

Suppose a game of musical chairs is being played. There are ten chairs, ten people, and you are the eleventh who are playing this game. Ten people can be symbolic of the ten vices of the mind such as anger, greed, hatred, lust, ego, etc. 'You' stands for the real you—the Self. As the game progresses, one by one people get 'out', i.e. the vices go on reducing with your spiritual practice. In the end only one chair and two people remain—you and ego. Both of you are running around the chair, and as soon as the music stops, both of you try to sit on the chair. Sometimes ego pushes you down and sometimes you push it down. A tussle goes on. The one, whose strength is more, wins. Sometimes you win and sometimes ego wins. When you win, you are in God space. When ego wins, you are on the time scale. This means you cannot enter the space of present with ego. When you surrender the ego, you enter the divine space.

Your ultimate aim should be to abide in the divine space, in the present. And remember you can either *think* or *be* in the present. Because, as soon as you think, you are not present in the present. So, being in the present is important.

Thus, when you enter the present through the point or hole between the past and future, you discover that the present is not on the time scale, it is behind time. It's endless and infinite. In fact the whole time scale, and even the whole universe, is in the present. When the Experiencer (Self) experiences the experience of *being* (Self), it is in the present. The present swallows up the past and future. Then there is nothing besides the present. Hence you may have heard that there is no past or future, only the present.

"Who am I now?" is a practice that will help you to enter the present. It is 'Enquiry in the Now,' where whatever is happening now (in the present moment) is used to shift back to the Self.

Q. 5 : So, I have to practice "Who am I now?" whenever I face any negative situation or get any negative thoughts?

What is ideal is to practice 'Enquiry of the Self' through the question "Who am I?" whenever and wherever you can. With 'Enquiry of the Now,' you are adding the word 'now' to the question "Who am I?" to check what you are identified with in the present moment and detach from it, so that you can return to your original state.

Therefore you should ask "Who am I now?" whenever the mind is caught in anything that takes you away from your original state—be it excitement or negative thoughts or situations. However, you would remember to ask "Who am I now?" when it is needed, only when you have had enough practice of asking this question beforehand. A good way to do so is to ask this question at hourly intervals throughout the day, say at 7:07, 8:08, 9:09, 10:10, 11:11… right from morning, with almost a gap of an hour.

Q. 6 : Why do you suggest that? And why 7:07, 8:08, and so on?

It is recommended to practice Self enquiry for a good period of time continuously in the morning. You will then enter your daily life as the real you. But along the way, you may get caught up in negative thoughts or situations, and forget your true nature. You need to ask yourself, "Who am I now?" at that time. But you may or may not remember that, hence it is good to have a solid plan.

If you are told to practice "Who am I now?" enquiry every hour, you may say yes, but may not actually do it. So, a unique time set is recommended. This time is when the hour and minute on the clock are the same. Thus, the recommended time slots throughout the day are as follows: 06:06 am, 07:07 am, 08:08 am… 12:12 pm, 01:01 pm, 02:02 pm…You can use technology to remind you by setting the alarm for these timings on your cell phone, computer, or any other gadget of your choice.

If you wake up at 6 in the morning and practice Self enquiry during that hour, then your Enquiry in the Now will begin at 7:07, and if you retire for sleep around 10 at night, then 10:10 will be your last time slot for the day. You need not wake up at night at 12:12, 1:01, etc. You are already one with the Self during deep sleep.

These particular times are being suggested because they have a rhythm about them. Everything in nature works in a rhythm. By following these rhythmic times, you will start getting tuned to the rhythm of nature as well as time. As a result your enquiry will also become tuned with time. Therefore this practice can be called as Time-Tuned Enquiry in the Now.

Q. 7 : That's great! How should I practice asking "Who am I now?" in a time-tuned manner?

Let's understand how to practice it in 3 simple steps:

Step 1 — Who was I?

As soon as your alarm goes off, say at 7:07 or 8:08, stop whatever you are doing for some time. This will apply a temporary break to your daily grind. Then sit down and close your eyes for two minutes. If the situation is such that you cannot sit or close your eyes, you can do it in whatever position your body is and with eyes open. Then ask yourself, "Who was I during the preceding hour?" Take a look at all the incidents that occurred during the previous hour and what you were identified with. Were you identified with being a "manager" or a "father" or a "smart guy" or a "beautiful girl" or any of your personality traits? You can also check against the A-L list that you learnt in Enquiry of the Mind. The idea is to check whether you had been considering yourself to be a separate individual or the infinite Self.

Step 2 — Who am I now?

Once you have reviewed the hour that has gone by, you can say, "I was a stressed / angry/ fearful… individual some time back, but, who am I now?" This will bring you to the present moment and remind you of your true nature. Attempt to locate the 'I' just like you have learnt in Self enquiry. In this process the mind will drop and you will shift to your experience of *being*. Stay in that experience for a few moments.

Step 3 — Who am I going to be?

Being in that experience, decide: "Who am I going to be during the next hour—the body-mind or the Self? Whatever is going to happen in the next hour, in all incidents how will I continue to be peaceful and operate from the Self?" With the intention to be established in the Self throughout the next hour, you will return to your normal routine as your true self. Thereafter try to maintain that state as long as possible. After an hour and a minute, you will repeat the same three steps again.

Q. 8 : What if we forget or are unable to carry out this enquiry at a particular time?

Let us suppose you practiced this enquiry at 01:01 pm and then could not practice it at 02:02 pm and then again remembered at 03:03 pm. Then at 03:03 pm look at the past two hours instead of the past hour. Also, suppose you know at 03:03 pm that your meeting will go on for the next 90 minutes and you will not be able to practice the enquiry at 04:04 pm, then decide how you will spend the next two hours.If you forget to practice enquiry at say 06:06 but remembered at 06:30, then practice it the moment you remember, and then get back to the schedule at 07:07 pm.

The idea of giving you a specific method is so that while you stay in the framework, you can tweak the details. What you should know is that thousands of seekers have reported that when they began practicing the time-tuned Enquiry in the Now at 01:01, 02:02, etc. it was much easier for them to remember to do it. Generally saying that they will do it every hour has not proven to be helpful to various seekers.

Using common sense, you won't be practicing this enquiry when you are crossing a busy street, driving in traffic, or operating machinery that cannot be stopped at that time. If you are unable to do it at certain times, don't worry about it or feel guilty. It's fine if, say out of 14 times, you are able to do it about 10 times. But you should try to practice it whenever possible throughout your waking hours. If you are unable to do it for 2 minutes, then it's okay to do it for a minute, and if you have more time, you can do it for 3-4 minutes.

After practicing vigorously for some days, you will start

noticing that automatically your attention goes to the clock when it is 2:02, 3:03, etc. However, if your attention goes to the clock and it is 2:01 or 3:02, don't say you still have a minute; start doing it because you may or may not have the time to do it later. The most important thing is to do it. Remember that the purpose of this time-tuned Enquiry in the Now is to develop the habit of asking "Who am I now?", so that once you have developed the habit, you can ask it whenever you are faced with negative situations or thoughts.

Q. 9 : What are the benefits of this time-tuned Enquiry in the Now?

'Enquiry in the now' done in a time-tuned manner is highly beneficial in the following ways:

1) It helps you to incorporate this powerful practice in your daily life. People always say they don't have time for anything, let alone for spiritual practice. But with this method, time itself will help you to shift onto your real self. You will get tuned with time and start finding time to help you do what you came to do on Earth: attain Self realization and stabilization.

2) Some seekers feel that once they have done their spiritual practice in the morning, it's enough. But if you are a serious seeker and want to attain stabilization, then the morning ritual is simply not enough. You have to maintain that practice throughout the day. This method will help you do that.

3) It helps you to develop discipline over your body-mind. What's wonderful is that after a few months of vigorous practice, it will become a part of your auto-system. That means it will become automatic for you and you won't have to put in much effort. Thereafter, even other activities will start happening on time, because you are tuned with time.

4) It effectively combines Mind's enquiry and Self enquiry.

5) It will raise your awareness about the tendencies, habits, thoughts, or emotions that usually arise in your body-mind. With awareness about the previous hour, you will enter the next hour with heightened awareness, due to which the possibility of getting entangled in the trap of those tendencies or situations will go on reducing. You will start getting liberated from the contrast mind.

6) It will easily and speedily shift you from various situations and states to the present moment.

7) It will make it easier to remember your true nature even during negative situations or while having negative thoughts. Thus, you can easily shift from negativity to your radiant self.

8) By frequently shifting to the Self, you will fall in love with the Self. That is Self-love. That is divine devotion. You will experience wonderment and sing praises on witnessing the divine play of the Self.

9) By remembering your true nature and dipping into it at frequent intervals, you will start being in that experience more and more. You will start being more of your true self and less of the body-mind. The idea is to progress towards Self stabilization—the state in which you will always be your true self. That is being in eternal bliss. That's the experience that the great saints like the Buddha or Mahavira were in.

Q. 10 : Wow! That's what every true seeker wants. There is one more question I wanted to ask. What exactly is the difference between Enquiry of the Self and Enquiry in the Now? In other words, what is the difference between asking "Who am I?" and "Who am I now?"

"Who am I now?" is an easy way of remembering to enquire. It is an extension of Enquiry of the Self. The word 'now' is an addition so that 'deletion' can begin. By making Self enquiry immediate and throughout the day with the question "Who am I now?", your ego is getting deleted, your identification with the body-mind is getting deleted, your habit of vacillating between the past and the future is getting deleted. With repeated practice of "Who am I now?" you will find that after a period of time, just the word "Who" is enough. Just one word—and Consciousness returns onto itself.

In Enquiry of the Now, you are doing Enquiry of the Self as

well. The only thing changing is the starting point. The addition of the word 'now' forces you to become aware of what you are identified with and use the answer to the question "Who am I now?" to shift back to the Self. Essentially it brings together Enquiry of the Mind and Enquiry of the Self. If you understand the essence of this practice, you can tweak the practice.

• • •

*You may reach the point of Self realization,
but if you don't work on eliminating
your tendencies and vices,
they prevent you from reaching
or getting established in the Self.*

6
ENDING THE ILLUSION

Q. 1 : You have imparted three wonderful techniques 'Enquiry of the mind,' 'Enquiry of the Self,' and 'Enquiry in the Now.' What is the essence of it all?

Let us understand the essence of Enquiry through a story. There is a well-known tale in Indian mythology about a demon called Bhasmasura.

Bhasmasura was a devotee of Lord Shiva and he performed great penance to obtain a boon from the Lord. Lord Shiva was pleased with his penance and ready to bestow a boon. Bhasmasura asked for immortality, but Shiva said this wish cannot be granted. Bhasmasura then asked that he be granted the power that anyone whose head he touched with his hand would be reduced to ashes (*bhasma*). Lord Shiva granted this request. Bhasmasura was delighted and could not wait to test his new power on someone. He suddenly got the thought that with this boon he was more powerful than even Lord

Shiva, and so he might as well try it on the Lord himself! He attempted to touch the head of Shiva. Astounded by Bhasmasura's audacity but tied by his own boon, Lord Shiva fled from the scene with Bhasmasura in hot pursuit. Shiva tried to get help from various gods but to no avail. While Shiva was being incessantly chased, he somehow managed to lose the demon for some time and rushed to Lord Vishnu to seek a solution to this predicament. Vishnu, on hearing Shiva's problem, agreed to help him out.

Vishnu, in the form of Mohini—a beautiful damsel—appeared before Bhasmasura. Mohini was so enchanting that Bhasmasura instantly fell in love with her and asked her to marry him. Mohini laughed and said, "Oh! You want to marry me? You should know that I am a dancer and when I was younger I made a promise that I would only marry a man who can dance as well as me."

Bhasmasura blinked. He had never danced in his whole life. But he promised himself that he would learn how to dance just to marry this woman.

Mohini looked at him and said anxiously, "Don't worry, I will teach you. If you follow my steps exactly the way I do it, I am yours and I will marry you." Well, he was ready to slay dragons for her.

So, the two of them danced. Bhasmasura tried his best to copy Mohini's moves as she smiled encouragingly at him. They went on dancing, and Bhasmasura got better and better at copying her moves. He concentrated on dancing and on nothing else. Mohini soon had a move where she kept her hand on her head. Without thinking Bhasmasura did the same!

Unfortunately for Bhasmasura, his powers worked... and he was reduced to ashes.

Q. 2 :   What a story! Does it symbolize the end of ego?

Yes, but let us understand the nuances. In this story, the demon Bhasmasura symbolizes the contrast mind, which judges and doubts everyone and everything, but never doubts itself. It never gets a thought that maybe it is the cause of sorrow. Because of its habit of constantly judging, comparing, doubting, blaming, and so forth, it becomes strong. In fact it becomes so strong and powerful that it tries to obliterate the Self (Lord Shiva in this story). Only with the help of Self enquiry (Lord Vishnu in this story), the mind begins to doubt itself and think, "Who feels miserable? Who is the one that burns with hatred and anger? Who is the one that wants to become dominant and powerful?" With this enquiry, it will keep its hand on its head and it will be annihilated, just like Bhasmasura. The Self behind it will then begin to shine. This is the essence of all three practices of enquiry—to use a 'thought' to annihilate all thoughts.

If you are practicing Self enquiry, you will understand the meaning of this story very well. You will realize, "Till date I had not realized, who was I assuming to be me? Whose sorrow was I considering to be mine? Whose joy was I believing to be mine? I was miserable only due to this misconception."

When you come to know "Who am I?" at the experiential level, then the contrast mind will drop (Bhasmasura will be obliterated). You may have experienced that when you enquired, "Who is feeling sorrow? Let me have a look within," then whom do you find? No one. You don't find anyone within who is sorrowful. The thought of sorrow appeared due to the contrast mind, you enquired about it, and the thought vanished… the thoughtless state manifested. Just like that. So simple. The contrast mind vanishes, but then it appears again. It again vanishes and again appears. This dance goes on, until the contrast mind is full obliterated. You have already started on this path.

Q. 3 : **That's good. I have understood that I am not the mind. Now how can I practically understand that I am also not the body?**

With the experiment that follows, you will be able to understand that you are also not the body; the body is merely your companion.

Read the following experiment, then put the book down and try this experiment right away. Before that you ought to understand that you are using the body, you are not the body. When you wear your clothes, you never say, "I am these clothes," you always say, "These are my clothes." You are not those objects with which you associate the words 'my' or 'mine' (E.g. my house, my eyes…). In order to understand this better, try the following experiment.

Look at your right hand for some time. After looking at it,

ask yourself, "Am I this hand?" Wait until you get the answer from within. The answer should be based on what you are experiencing and not using the intellect. Give this a minute. Look at your hand and ask yourself, "Am I this hand?" What association do you experience with your hand? Ask yourself again, "Am I this hand?" Then look at the hand carefully. You will probably experience, "This hand is mine, but I am not this hand." In the same way, conduct this experiment with all other parts of the body (leg, torso, face, back, etc.). Repeat this question for each part of the body that you are able to see: "Am I this foot? Am I this stomach?" You can also try this experiment while looking into the mirror. With this experiment, you get the feeling, "If I am not all of this, then who indeed am I?!"

Next, ask the question, "Suppose this hand is cut off, then will I continue to exist? Will I still feel complete from within or not?" Wait for the answer. You will probably get the answer, "I will still continue to exist; I will still be complete." The experience from within will tell you, "I am complete. In spite of losing a hand, I do not feel incompleteness within."

Some people lose their limbs in accidents; yet they say, "I exist." They never say, "I am incomplete now, earlier I was complete." This is because when your body is cut, *you* do not get cut. When you start experiencing this truth, then the root of all false beliefs 'I am the body' will break. You can experience your true self.

Q. 4 : Wow! What a simple and powerful way to

experience that I am not the body. I have already experienced that I am not the mind with Enquiry of the mind. With Enquiry of the Self and Enquiry in the Now, I have experienced the Self. This means I have attained Self realization. Doesn't this mean I have reached the destination of my spiritual journey?!

This is not the destination. It is essential to attain complete knowledge. The most important knowledge is understanding your true nature at the experiential level. This is Self realization. But is that all? No. After Self realization, you have to see whether your body is allowing you to stay in the experience of Self or not? Is it supporting you to abide in your true nature? If it does, then you will get established or stabilized in the Self, which is called Self stabilization.

Thus Self realization and Self stabilization are two different things. You may reach the point of Self realization, but what happens with people on reaching this point? Until a truth seeker has not experienced the Self even once, he carries on with his quest vigorously with enthusiasm and sincerity. He puts in all his strength. He wants to understand who he actually is. He is eager to know what the experience of *being* is. He has heard praises being sung about it, he has read what Lord Buddha or Lord Mahavira has said about it. He wonders, what is it? What have all the saints achieved? Saint Tukaram sang beautiful hymns, Saint Kabir expounded the most exquisite couplets, Saint Mira was lost in devotional songs and dance, and Jesus even accepted the cross. The seeker has a burning desire to know, what had they attained? So he continues the journey diligently and carries out his spiritual practice with perseverance, putting in everything he has. Finally one day he reaches the experience of Self. He is ecstatic. But once he has touched the experience, his contrast mind says, "Now I know. I have experienced the Self." The individual considers it to be its achievement and tells everybody about it.

And what happens after that? If the body has wrong tendencies, habits, or patterns, then these do not allow him to go onto the Self again. In fact these obstacles stop him and his mind gives excuses. On the other hand, if these obstacles do allow him to reach the Self, they pull him back very soon.

Q. 5 : Oh! That means wrong tendencies and habits prevent spiritual growth?

Absolutely. To get a clear picture, let us consider an analogy.

Suppose you are in a big hall. Now imagine that you have been tied to one end of the hall with a huge rubber band from behind. You are then told that you have to reach the other end of the hall—that's where lies the experience of Self. You have heard that the experience is the most beautiful of all experiences; in fact religions have been formed based on that experience. Hence you are keen to experience it. You marshal all your strength, move forward against the resistance of the rubber band, and reach the Self. You feel so happy that at last you have experienced it.

However, the next time you want to reach the experience, you have the thought in your mind that you have already experienced it once. What does the rubber band symbolize?

It symbolizes your tendencies and habits that pull you back. You are trying to move forward but are feeling the pull from behind. You had felt the pull the first time around too, but then you had great attraction for the experience. But now that you have already experienced it, your attraction has decreased a bit, and at the first sign of resistance, you say, "Ok, I will do it tomorrow. Looks like I am not in the right mood today... Guests are going to arrive and I have a lot of work... As it is, I have already experienced it once. It is within me, and I can access it whenever I want." Every time you try to reach the experience, the tendencies pull you back and you drop the idea. Although sometimes you are able to reach the experience, but because of the thought that you have already experienced it, you go on reducing your efforts.

This is just like a person who has already visited a picnic spot and is now going for it the second time. The level of attraction is not the same. This time this person is with friends who would be visiting for the first time. Due to some problems on the way, it looks like the journey has to be aborted. He says that they should turn back, while his friends feel they should continue the journey despite the obstacles. However, he feels that he has already seen it once; so why strive to reach it again in the face of difficulties? He does not know the importance of going there again and again. Also he is unaware that he does not have to just reach that place, he also needs to stay there for a period of time. He has to experience what happens and what thoughts he gets when he stays there.

Likewise, you may not be aware that you don't have to just touch the experience of *being* and come back. You are supposed to stay in that experience, you have to experience what happens when you stay in that state —what kind of thoughts you get in that state, how is it at day and how is it at night, how is it during various seasons, and what do you come in contact with in that state. This can happen only when you stay in that experience. Hence the need to eliminate vices and develop discipline, so that the body can support you to access the experience repeatedly and stay there for a longer time.

Thus, if you haven't worked on reducing and eliminating your tendencies and vices, they prevent you from reaching the Self. In addition to tendencies, the obstacles may be patterns, emotional blockages, memories of the past, sorrowful or vengeful feelings for someone you haven't been able to forgive, and so on. A seeker may start thinking that having attended a spiritual retreat, he has become wise and even attained Self realization, and hence he can go and teach the people who had troubled him a lesson or two. He feels he can face them confidently and they should know whom they are dealing with now. The ego that "I am knowledgeable" also gets added to the list of obstacles. Gradually one gets entangled once again in the web of the mind and its games. Consequently one is unable to experience the Self. Hence it is imperative to work on purifying your body-mind of all the obstacles.

Q. 6 : How do I work on purifying and training my body-mind?

You have to start working on eliminating your tendencies

bit by bit. These tendencies can be that of wrong habits, vices, addictions, judging, blaming, labeling everything, always assuming oneself to be right, giving too much value to one's emotions, justifying one's habit of emotionally blackmailing others, etc. Getting rid of these tendencies bit by bit will purify your body-mind.

Continue practicing enquiry as described earlier, regularly and diligently. It is highly effective in purifying and training your body-mind. Spiritual practices such as forgiveness are also very helpful in purification. You need to forgive people and seek forgiveness (at least mentally), let go of the past, accept your body, and accept whatever has happened. Do not hold onto things such as, this person did this to me and that person did that. Now look at everyone with a new eye. Let the old thinking and memories stop influencing you. Liberate yourself from the past. You will then become like a child—who is always in the experience of Self and always in the present moment.

When your tendencies and patterns break, and you are constantly on the Self, it means you have moved beyond the three states into the fourth state—*turiya*, and from there you can proceed towards the *turiyateet* state.

Q. 7 :   I have heard about *turiya* and *turiyateet* states. Can you please elaborate on them?

In the physical dimension of this world, you pass through three states every day: wakefulness, sleep, and dreams. You keep shuffling between these states. By now you are already aware that you are not the body. Although you are presently in the physical dimension, you are not a physical being. The dimension that you actually belong to is not in this world, it is beyond this world and its three states. That is the fourth state, which is called as the turiya state. The mind will not be able to understand that state or dimension. The mind exists in the physical dimension and its three states. It does not exist in the other dimension or the fourth state.

The real you enters the physical dimension from the fourth state. You keep shuffling between the three states, but totally miss out going back to the fourth state, to reach the real you. The whole point of spirituality is to take you back to that state. You need to realize that wherever you are or whatever you are doing in this world, you are actually not in this place or in these activities. You are outside everything. Developing this conviction is important. When you are convinced, you won't get stuck in the happenings of this worldly illusion. Now you get entangled in them because you think that you are in this world, you are of this world.

This is because you did not remind yourself and experience your true self, while entering this world in the morning. If you had, you wouldn't have got stuck in the happenings of this world. And if you did remind yourself and are still getting stuck, it means you did not do it properly. That is why it is recommended to ask yourself "Who am I?" 40-50 times vigorously in the morning with every thought that arises. However, if you did that properly and yet get stuck, it means you forgot about it during the various happenings of the day. That means you have to remind yourself several times throughout the day. The question "Who am I now?" makes this possible.

The thought 'Who am I?' or 'Who am I now?' does not belong to the physical dimension nor to the other dimension. In fact it is the one that can connect the two dimensions. It is not of the physical dimension because it connects you to the other dimension. And it is not of the other dimension because there are no thoughts in that dimension.

While this may sound mystical, the reason of stating it is to bring forth the power of enquiry. Once you are convinced that the power of this thought is enormous and this question can connect you to the fourth state, you shall be consistent in your practice. Since you forget it when you ask just once, hence you will ask this question many times. Every time you ask it, you wait for some time for the answer. You try to locate the 'I'. Slowly you begin to connect to the fourth state. Then you have to operate from that state throughout the day.

The fourth (*turiya*) state is connected to the three states, through which the fourth state experiences itself. However, there is one more state which is beyond these four states—*turiyateet* (beyond the fourth). When the turiya state is not connected to the three states, when it is not experiencing itself through the three states, when it is pure essence 'at rest'—then it is the fifth state or turiyateet. People read these ancient terms and may or may not understand their meaning, hence here is a contemporary example that may help.

Suppose our original state (fourth state) puts on make-up. The three states are its make-up. We know the fourth state only with make-up; we haven't known it without make-up. Imagine there is someone who has taken the appearance of a clown with all the make-up including the dress and the hat, and has presented before you. But the one who is inside the make-up must exist even without this dress and make-up, right? That is the fifth state—turiyateet. Thus, that which is present with the three states is the turiya state, although it has the make-up of the three states upon it. When this make-up is removed, that's the fifth state.

Q. 8 :   How can we know this fifth state?

Obviously the mind cannot know the fifth state too. However, you have to develop conviction about that state. It's conviction that counts the most. If you are convinced, then you will lead your life accordingly. You have to develop this conviction about the fifth state in this (physical) dimension itself, in the wakeful state. Hence the need of a spiritual master (Guru), the need for faith, and need for devotion. This is because the highest things cannot be understood with the intellect. One cannot understand even the fourth state, then how can one comprehend the fifth state? You cannot recognize it *with* make-up, then how will you recognize it *without* make-up?

When you attain a true master, you should focus on the conviction with which your master tells you about the fourth and fifth states, so that you too develop the same conviction and recognize your true self. The external guru is to help you reach the internal guru (Self). You have to learn to recognize yourself without the make-up, although at present you are in make-up.

From childhood we have seen only the make-up of the three states. After a child is born, it lives only in these three states, it is not even aware that there is a state beyond these three states. But there is such a state and its conviction can be developed. To do so, you have to carry out certain experiments. One of them is Self enquiry. You can ask, "Who am I?" while beginning your day as described earlier and then throughout the day, you can remind yourself by asking, "Who am I now?" This question will repeatedly connect you to the fourth state, so that you can attain the conviction about the fifth state—which is without make-up, which is formless. The mind can never know it. But with repeated Enquiry of the Self and Enquiry in the Now, you can develop the conviction that such a state exists.

Q. 9 : What is the importance of developing that conviction?

When you develop that conviction, you witness all the events in your life with ease and bliss. Thus, your life itself will show whether you have done your spiritual practice in the right manner or not and whether you have developed the conviction of your true nature or not. If you haven't, then you have to start doing it. Ask for forgiveness from the Self if it feels difficult to carry out your spiritual practice, and thereby clear the path for your practice. And why will you carry out the practice? Because you have understood its importance.

All the thoughts are of this world, there is only one thought which is of beyond this world, and you have come to know of it. That's a reason for great happiness! Sometimes you may have a rare diamond in your hand, but may not be aware of its value. Hence you may not use it to its potential. But now that you are aware that it can lead you to your supreme self, you will start thinking whether you are using it or not.

And all through the day, you will ask "Who am I now?" at intervals such as 1:01, 2:02, and so on. This will make you aware of what tendencies, thoughts, blames, judgments, complaints had come up during the preceding hour, which pull you away from your happy natural state and bind you into a coffin. You then wait for the Judgment Day to be released from the coffin and for justice to be dispensed. But justice has been served to you. You don't need to live in the coffin of unwanted beliefs and tendencies. Start living openly. Whenever some thought or somebody puts you in a coffin with certain words or behavior, simply come out by asking, "Who am I now?" You are formless and boundless, who can bind you if you don't allow it? You are out of the box. People say, "Think out of the box." You will say, "I am out of the box." Whatever the Self or God* thinks, it will be out of the box.

• • •

---

*You can read *Enquiry about God and Beliefs* in Appendix-I of this book.

You receive the Popular Mantra
"I am the body" in various forms right from childhood,
and hence start believing yourself to be the body.
The Forgotten Mantra will remind you of your essence
and take you back to your heaven home.

EPILOGUE

Once upon a time, there lived some people in a highly evolved society. They were highly evolved beings who knew the truth that God alone exists in everyone and everything; and there are no separate individuals. They led their lives living this supreme truth. They all lived in total bliss and harmony.

In this society, there was a beautiful neighborhood called Heaven Home. In Heaven Home, there lived a boy called Rama. One day, a thought popped up in Rama's mind: "Can my shadow come alive?" This thought created great excitement as well as turmoil within him. He couldn't stop thinking about it and finally asked his parents, "Can my shadow come alive? I want to play with it and always enjoy its company." Listening to this strange question, his parents got worried and took him to see a doctor.

The doctor was astonished by the boy's question. He said, "All these years I have never had a patient who wanted their shadow to come alive. This boy cannot be treated for it in this place. He can be cured only in the city."

His parents immediately sent him to the city to get him treated as soon as possible. However, the boy reached the city and again started asking people, "This is my shadow and I want it to come alive. What should I do for that?" People told him, "It's no big deal. You can go to this *ashram* and you will get the solution." The boy gladly went to the said ashram. There he found a priest and expressed his wish. The priest said, "There is a Popular Mantra. On repeating it, your wish will be fulfilled."

The specialty of this city was that all the people used this mantra. Whenever they faced any problem, they would chant this mantra.

As suggested by the priest, the boy constantly chanted the popular mantra while gazing at his shadow. He sometimes got bored or tired by the constant repetition. He would then go and meet the priest, who would then suggest a new method of chanting the mantra. Once the priest told him, "You have to chant this mantra at least a thousand times a day. When you have chanted it 84,00,000 times, your shadow will come alive."

With renewed vigor, the boy started chanting the mantra day and night. When he had finished chanting the recommended number of times, his shadow actually came alive! The popular mantra had worked. After that the boy started living there with his shadow. He would play with it and was content. He never returned to Heaven Home.

The story does not end here. But let us now understand the symbolism of this story. What is the Popular Mantra? What is Heaven Home? What is the city?

This story indicates that initially the boy used to live in his home (at his centre—in the experience of *being*) and was happy. But then a desire arose inside him to make his shadow come alive. That is why he was sent away from the highly evolved society into the city. Just like when somebody develops an infectious disease, they are sent into quarantine, so as to prevent the spread of the disease. The same was suggested by the doctor and the boy was sent away to the city, just as Adam and Eve were sent to Earth, away from their home in paradise.

The desire for the shadow to come alive was like an infectious disease, and to prevent other people from getting such ideas, it was essential to send him away. There is no place for such people in a highly evolved society. Hence they are sent away to the city. Because in the city there are already many people whose shadow has come alive by chanting the Popular Mantra.

In the ashram of the city, even little children of two-and-a-half or three years are initiated into this mantra. You may be a bit baffled by this story but you will understand it clearly upon knowing the meaning of the popular mantra. So, what was the Popular Mantra? What were the words that he repeated millions of times? The words were: "I am the body." This made his shadow (body) come alive.

This story is not of somebody else. It is *your* story. As a little child, you always live in your experience of *being*, i.e. you live in Heaven Home. Then, when you are two-and-a-half or three years old, you start receiving the popular mantra. This means you start listening to all the people around you who speak to you considering themselves to be the body. Looking at them, you too start regarding yourself to be the body. Also everybody always speaks to you as if you are the body. In this way, you are constantly hammered that you are the body and you chant this mantra millions of times. After such repetition, you firmly believe yourself to be the body, which has been stated as the shadow coming alive in the story.

You are regarding yourself to be the body, and the individual ego that got created due to that, you are playing with that ego. The ego means the sense of separateness or individuality. That ego keeps on saying something throughout the day, such as, "He did this… she did that… that person did this to you…" In this way you are living with the individual ego.

Just think about it, are you ever alone? The one who is speaking from inside you is the individual ego or your shadow. The only thing is, you forgot that the individual thoughts going on within you are actually your shadow; they are not you. And it is you who made the shadow come alive; although in ignorance. The reality is that every person receives the Popular Mantra by the age of two-and-a-half to three years. It is a popular mantra because everybody is repeating it. Otherwise mantras are not easy to get and are consequently lost, just as what happened with the Forgotten Mantra.

Rama, who had learnt the popular mantra in the city, if he happens to remember his Heaven Home and wishes to return to it, what should he do? He would need a new mantra, which is called the Forgotten Mantra. He should have remembered and used the Forgotten Mantra and returned home, but he was content living with his shadow. That is why he could never return home.

This is what happens with man. He gets entangled in the city (material world or *maya*) so much that he fails to remember that he needs to return to his Heaven Home. Very few people return to their Heaven Home (the Source or experience of *being*). If you want to return to your experience of *being*, remember the Forgotten Mantra.

The good news is that you have already learnt that mantra earlier in the book, which is: "Who am I now?" Use it at every instance and return to your true nature.

The message that you have been given in this book is: Do not get stuck in your body or that of others. Make your body an instrument for the expression of the Self everywhere you go. Your body is your temple, hence turn within and view the Self or God constantly. This wisdom is such that it will liberate you from the old, from ignorance, turmoil, tendencies, slavery of the mind, as well as from every false belief.

For this to happen, you need to detach yourself from the Popular Mantra ('I am the body'), even if it is highly popular. Even if everybody is always using it. Even if it is always the reference point used by everybody in every aspect.

Whenever anybody is speaking with the body as the reference point, such as, "I met my sister" or "Your hair looks good," say in your mind, "Who am I now?" and shift to your *being*. So, the other person may be conversing in accordance with the popular mantra, but you will continue to remember your true self. You will listen while being in the experience of your true self. Thus, you will be able to detach from your shadow (body-mind, individual ego). Since so many years you have been leading your life assuming yourself to be the body and hence you have forgotten that you are separate from it. The Forgotten Mantra will remind you of the truth.

You have understood that within all the people of the world —rich or poor, black or white, belonging to any religion or community—God alone exists. This book gives you the proof. If you attain the right understanding, you can then remember the golden words: *God alone exists; ascertain whether you exist or not.* You can make this understanding a part of your life. Whether you are at home or at work, you can see God in everyone. Seeing God in every being is attaining supreme wisdom.

Suppose your brother is sleeping and somebody comes and asks you, "Who is this?" You will naturally say, "This is my brother." If that person tells you, "How can he be your brother? He is sleeping." You will reply right back, "So what if he is sleeping? He is still my brother." In the same way, God is asleep in some people, but it is still God.

In some bodies, God is a bit unconscious, or intoxicated, or in coma, but that does not prove that God does not exist in them. If a body is alive, it directly means that God is present in it. Only the state of God varies in different bodies. Unconsciousness and ignorance vanish on attaining wisdom and God manifests in its original state in that body. If you are able to see God in even one person, you can then see God in everyone—whatever state God may be in. If there is someone in your life that you do not like, you can pray, "May God start operating more openly and fully in that body." The words can vary, but by praying in this manner, you will eventually start seeing God in that person too. And just as there is God in everyone, remember that God is present in you too.

When one has not understood fully, one may start considering the body to be God. However, it is the consciousness, the living entity, the experience of Self or *being* that is God. It is erroneous if an individual starts believing, "I am God." The reality is that no body is God. The body is a corpse, it is non-living or insentient. The consciousness permeating the body is God. It is possible to be mistaken when one forgets the truth. Hence always continue to remind yourself: God alone exists. Ascertain whether you exist or not. The mantra, "Who am I now?" will help you in remembering.

● ● ●

APPENDIX - I

You can attain God
not just by believing,
thinking, or knowing about God,
but by *being*.

ENQUIRY ABOUT GOD AND BELIEFS

Q. 1 : Does God exist?

An atheist will say "God does not exist" and a theist will say "God exists." Both have incomplete knowledge. The truth is *God alone exists; there is nothing or none other than God.* Whether God exists or not, is a baseless question. Suppose you ask a person who is lying down, "Are you awake?" If he says "yes," it means he is awake. Even if he says "no," it still means that he is awake. In the same way, if a person says "God exists," it means that God exists. Even if the person says "God does not exist," it still means that God exists. Because even to be able to say "no," the body should be operated by an enlivening principle, which is God (or whatever name you want to give). Who is it that is saying, "God does not exist"? It is Him alone! God alone exists; ascertain and confirm whether you exist.

Q. 2 : Who is God?

Every one lives with the belief that God has created man. But the reality is that God did not create man, God became man! The 'real I' or your original essence, which is ever present, is God.

There is that 'I' which others think I am. There is that 'I' which I think myself to be. There is that 'I' which I want to become in the future. All these are false 'I's or false notions. You are not what others perceive you to be. You are not what you perceive yourself to be or the one that you want to be in the future. The one who perceives within you is the 'real I'. When you experience the real I and understand that the false I is merely a thought, you attain Self realization. When you experientially know the real I, you know God. Both are one and the same.

Q. 3 : Oh!! So I am God?

The real I is God, the body is not God. The formless, universal, omnipresent I is the real I. This real I is God. Clearly understand that your body-mind-intellect is not the real I, so it is not God. This real I is nothing but the Universal Self.

Q. 4 : Who created God?

Sirshree : Do you think that God can die?

Seeker : No.

Sirshree : If something cannot die, how can it ever be created? God is and has always existed. It is beyond life and death. God is eternal life.

Q. 5 :   When did God create this world?

This question is related to time. However, the concept of time appeared after the world was created. Then how is it possible to answer this using a concept that came later? Or understand it in this way: the world was created when time began. But that which was before time is actually what is important, because it always existed and will continue to exist. Time is but a small aspect of it. A part cannot measure the whole. God is timeless, spaceless, and ageless.

Q. 6 :   What was there before the world was created? And how did God create this universal divine play (*lila*)?

When the world did not exist, then only the Self or God existed. God created this world only for experiencing Himself. This world is a mirror for God to witness Himself. Thus, the whole world, including everything living (including us) and non-living is just a medium for God to experience and express Himself.

Along the creation of the world, God also created the contrast mind as a part of His divine play. The contrast mind is the part of the mind that constantly compares, judges, and categorizes everything into good or bad. This is the mind that always lives either in the past or the future. When this contrast mind considers itself to be an individual that has a separate existence, that's when the divine game gets complicated. Man forgets who he actually is.

Until the appearance of man, the universe was functioning very easily and smoothly. With the creation of man and the contrast mind that makes man forget who he is, the game of seeking oneself began. This gave birth to Self enquiry. In reality, it is God searching for God. God searches for Himself and then finds Himself and experiences immense bliss (that's the game). This is called as Self realization, for which Self enquiry is essential.

Q. 7 : How can we understand the divine game?

Try to understand the divine game through an example. Suppose you are looking at a picture in which a man is watching a pigeon. In this context, the man is the seer, the pigeon is the seen, and the act occurring between them is seeing. But you are outside this picture, and for you, all three are part of one and the same picture.

Similarly when you find yourself outside the picture of this world, you realize, "I am just connected to this body-mind. The body-mind is seeing everything happening in this world. I am outside this whole picture. I am the Witness that is witnessing this body-mind which is looking and participating in this world."

In the olden days, there used to be bioscope shows. The bioscope was an early film projector, which was in the shape of a box and the size of an average television. It had 4-5 round windows, each with the diameter of about 4 inches. You could peep in through one of the windows to see the primitive movies that played in it. For modern times, we can consider a virtual reality headset, which is set over your eyes. While seeing the movies or games being played, you feel as if you are in there and get lost in them. This is because you can see an entire world inside with various people, buildings, and objects. You can see people coming out or going in the buildings. But you, who is peeping inside through the bioscope or the headset, are outside. You are neither inside the building nor outside. You are outside of inside and outside.

This world created by God is also like a movie playing inside the bioscope or a virtual reality game. But you have forgotten your true nature and are so lost in this world that you don't remember that you are outside the movie or the game. In this scenario, the character of a guru plays a very important role in your life. When the guru comes from behind and gives you a little smack on your head, you awaken out of your unconsciousness. You look behind and remember, "Oh! I am outside the bioscope (world). I am not in this illusionary world. A moment back I believed I was inside and was fighting with a friend—but that was all just an illusionary game." The guru's smack is essential for you to understand and develop this conviction. Initially people dislike the smack but later on they say that the knock was simply divine grace, which pulled them out of the divine play and awakened them to reality.

Q. 8 : **There are so many different names used for God throughout the world, but do they all imply the**

same?

Yes. God, Lord, Allah, *Ishwar*, Yahweh, Father, the Spirit, Super Consciousness, the Creator, the Almighty, Divinity, Universal Self, Self, *Waheguru, Moun* (eternal silence), Bright Witness, *Sat-Chit-Anand*—many names have been given by different people. However, they all imply the same.

Q. 9 :   But what is the actual name of God?

'Nameless Truth' is the name of God. Either all names are the names of God or none of the names is the name of God. Either all forms are the form of God or no form is the form of God. Whenever someone has proclaimed the truth to the world, they have chanted the name of God. The truth that existed even before any of the names of God were coined is the name of God. The truth that was chanted even before the birth of any incarnations or messengers of God is the name of God. Truth is God and God is truth.

If Nameless Truth is the name of God, then just chanting "Truth Truth" is also not true chanting. Only when you *think* the truth (which is beyond duality) does real chanting take place. 'Thinking the truth' and 'thinking about the truth' are two different things. When you read or think over stories of Gods of your religion, you are thinking about the truth, not thinking the truth. When someone says, "It is night," then in spite of being true, it is not the truth but a fact. To chant the truth or to think the truth is to enquire, "Who am I?" and experience it.

The name that leads you to the experience of *being* is the

name of God. On uttering any of the popular names of God, if you are reminded of the illusory world, then it is not the name of God. On the contrary, by uttering the name of a demon or any negative character, if you are reminded of the truth, then that is the name of God. Thus, it does not matter what name or word it is, the main thing is, it should lead you to the experience of God.

Q. 10 : How do you best describe God?

Let's understand this through a story.

A man came to a city and began speaking unheard things about God. This upset the people who heard him. They caught hold of him, took him to the King, and complained, "Your Majesty! This man is speaking something different about God." When asked for an explanation, the man said, "Your Majesty, I can prove that I am not misguiding anybody." To prove his point, he called three ministers and to each one of them he gave a packet of mud and said, "Describe the content of this packet without mentioning its name." The first minister said, "Everything is born out of this thing. This is that from which everything is created. The seeds of all trees are in it." The second minister described, "This is not water. Apart from water, whatever remains is this thing." The third one said, "This is that into which everyone will merge one day." Then the man revealed the secret... "Look! Even when asked about something as simple as mud, we had three different answers from three different people. Then just imagine how many different answers might have been given about God! If the answers are different, does it change the essence of God?" The King was convinced and set him free.

Thus, different answers can be given about God... God is nothing and the world emerged from nothingness. Just one seed can give rise to a forest. If you break the seed open, what do you find? Nothing! God is also nothing. This nothing is not the 'nothing' which we usually mean. It is everything. God is nothing with the potential of everything. God means the consciousness pervading everybody and everything. That, which is life, is God. While all these words can describe a little about what is God, yet it cannot be fully expressed in words. It has to be experienced.

Q. 11 : Where is God?

Sirshree : Choose from these three answers:

- God is present inside us
- God is outside us in the universe
- God is present both in and out.

Seeker : I guess it's the third one.

Sirshree : You are correct in a way, but actually God is beyond inside and outside.

When one learns that the Consciousness is within us, one might imagine that it exists within the body. And, though it may logically be considered correct, but the Consciousness is not just within the body. Rather, the body exists within the Consciousness (God). All of this existence is happening within the Consciousness (God).

Think of a fish living in water. Water is an all-pervading presence for the fish. It is the essential medium that keeps the fish alive. Water exists not only within the fish, but also all around it. Water is so close to its eyes that the fish doesn't realize that it's in water. What if the fish swam off in search of water, asking, "Where is water?"

This is precisely what the questioning mind would ask when it is told about the all-pervading nature of God: "Where is God?"

God or Consciousness is so close to you; in fact, it is your very essence. If you carefully observe, you will find that the spatial concepts of inside and outside are relative to your body and belong to the realm of the mind. From the standpoint of Consciousness, there is neither *inside* nor *outside*. Hence it is more correct to say that Consciousness or God is outside of inside and outside, which means God is limitless and is present everywhere.

Q. 12 : Then, where should we seek God?

Sirshree : You tell me. If God is both in and out and actually beyond in and out, then where should you seek God?

Seeker : Maybe 'in' would be easier.

Sirshree : Precisely. Our body is always with us and hence we can take a dip within anytime we want and get a glimpse of the divine. Even if you seek God outside, you will ultimately reach within. We look into the mirror (an external source), but all it does is reflect to us our own self. All idols and religious symbols exist for one reason alone—to take us within. Only then do temples serve their purpose.

Q. 13 : Where did God come from?

This sounds like a good question. But it presupposes that God was somewhere else and not here. If he came here, then he won't be where he was earlier. So, does he keep moving from one place to another? The fact is that God is everywhere (omnipresent). Where did God come from—this question itself is wrong. If someone asks you, "Is the color red crooked or straight?", you would say that red color has nothing to do with being crooked or straight. This question itself is wrong. Thus questions such as where did God come from and where he was are all in vain.

Q. 14 : Does God have form or is he formless?

God is the formless reality beyond the mind and intellect. Man makes use of his mind and intellect to understand everything. To start with, it is essential to show various pictures in order to teach a child. What are the pictures that can be shown to the beginners on the path of spirituality? Because no picture can be made of the Formless. But, taking the need into consideration, the mistake of creating pictures and idols was deliberately committed by some great masters. This mistake ends upon attaining Self realization because the essential purpose of the mistake then becomes clear.

Just as the eye needs the mirror as the means to see itself, God needs form as a means to know himself. The world is the form which is the need of the Formless. The world is that mirror which is the face of the Formless.

A new truth seeker cannot understand this. Hence he is presented two statements:

1. God has a form and becomes formless at times.
2. God is formless and assumes a form when he chooses to.

The seeker is asked which of the two statements is true. The second statement is the right answer. But what would a person of average intellect give more importance to—gold or gold ornaments? Of course, to ornaments! (Although in all gold ornaments, there is only one thing which is common—gold.) Thus they give more value to gold which has been given a shape. Similarly people give more importance to form. However, for the goldsmith, gold or golden ornaments are one and the same. A goldsmith sees gold in every gold ornament. The shape of the ornaments and the shapelessness of gold is the same thing for him. In the same way, form and formless are the same for those who have the understanding of God and truth.

Those who believe in form and those who believe in the formless are both watching the same movie. Some are watching the part of the movie before the interval and some are watching the part after the interval. After watching the movie, when both get a chance to discuss, they argue saying, "You are wrong." But the fact is that both of them have seen the same movie. 'Formless' is the form of God; 'attributeless' is the attribute of God.

Q. 15 : Is God male? What about the pictures of God?

God is beyond gender, color, and imagination. One day a teacher asked a student, "What is the color of the sky?" The student answered, "The sky is orange," for he had seen the sky at dusk. When the second student was asked, he replied, "The sky is black," since he had seen the sky at night. If we are asked the same question, we might say that the sky is blue.

Similarly a picture is formed in our minds as soon as someone utters the word "God." People who have been raised according to Hindu tradition imagine a masculine God wearing a crown and ornaments on his body. Similarly followers of Christianity would imagine God in the form of Jesus of Nazareth. This applies to many different religious traditions around the world. Such imaginations too become an obstacle in the quest for God.

Although some sects believe in goddesses, the predominant belief is that God is masculine. This has been passed down through generations and no one questions this aspect. These assumptions become an obstacle and we get entangled in our own assumptions.

If someone were to ask you "How does a doughnut look

like?", a ring shape would emerge before your mind's eye. You would never imagine a square doughnut. If a square doughnut was made, will the new shape change its taste? No. But our idea is so firm that we think a doughnut has to be ring-shaped.

Similarly we assume that God has to be masculine because we have seen His imaginary pictures in books, on calendars, and in movies. A quest for God based on such imaginations can never attain fulfillment.

Children in kindergarten are taught words. Along with words, pictures of the corresponding objects are also shown. The child learns the words by associating them with pictures. Looking at the pictures, his understanding rises, and in the future, he is able to understand the words without the associated pictures. Likewise, initially pictures of God are useful. Moving ahead, one can experience God even without pictures or idols. The seekers who advance from kindergarten realize that God is beyond form. God is—eternal, timeless, unborn, self existent, impregnable, constant, egoless, formless, attributeless, fearless, devoid of hatred, omnipresent, omnipotent, omniscient, spaceless, beyond the senses, and beyond the reach of the mind.

There are many preconceived ideas about God. The human mind can imagine about God, however, the mind can never experience God. Just as the eyeglasses cannot see the eye, similarly, the mind—which is the eyeglass of God— can never catch sight of God. When the mind gains the understanding of truth, it realizes that it is being the obstacle for the Self (God) to experience itself. The mind then surrenders and drops with this understanding, resulting into a thoughtless state. It is then that the Self (God) reveals itself. You then understand that God is beyond masculine or feminine. For convenience purposes, you may say "he" or "she" so long as you understand that God is beyond he, she, or it.

Q. 16: Why has God created both positive and negative aspects?

People always have this question that why did God create bad along with the good? Suppose you are told to write a novel and are instructed to have only positive characters in it. You will say, in that case how will the novel be interesting? Because unless there is a negative character or situation, a novel cannot be written. This is the first condition to create a novel. Both hero and villain are essential, otherwise one is incomplete without the other.

We always tend to look at an event from only one perspective and draw conclusions based upon it. We don't look at its other aspects. If God has made some people rich and some poor, there is definitely a reason behind it. If you really understand this, you will say, "This is exactly how it should be." Let us look at a little story to understand this. A man was always lamenting why God did not make everybody rich. One night he had a dream, in which he saw that a huge bag of money had appeared outside everybody's door. As soon as people discovered it, they were ecstatic. His happiness also knew no bounds. He went inside to deliver the good news, when his wife told him that their son had fallen sick. He ran to fetch the doctor. But the doctor wasn't available in his clinic and had left the note that he would no longer be working because he had lots of money and was going to enjoy it. Same was the case with other doctors too. He called his office to let them know he would be coming in late but there was nobody working in the office. When he returned home anxious and worried, his wife had some more bad news. Their maid had left the job because she no longer needed the money. The plumber would not come to repair the faucet, well, because he no longer needed to work. The construction workers working on their roof had abandoned the project too. The list was endless... he couldn't bear it anymore... and woke up with a cold sweat! With a breath of relief, he exclaimed, "Thank God, everybody is not rich!!"

Thus, if you really understand the supreme intelligence of the Creator, you will say, "This is exactly how it should be." Today honest people are valued due to the existence of many corrupt people. Today the truth is given importance because of widespread prevalence of deceit and lies. Unless you understand this, unless you have the eye to see the other aspect, you will continue to think that everything happening in this world is wrong.

A king was analyzing the economical condition of his kingdom. He discovered that a good part of grains is eaten up by the sparrows in the fields. The king got worried and started thinking of measures to prevent this loss. He declared that all the sparrows in the kingdom should be killed. He also announced that all those who killed sparrows will be rewarded according to the number of sparrows they kill. People rushed to kill as many sparrows as they could. Soon almost all the sparrows of the kingdom were eliminated. The king was pleased. He felt that he had solved the problem. But the next time he analyzed the reports, to his surprise he found that the production of grains had gone down even further. On investigation it was found that worms and insects were eating away the grains. The king had not considered that besides grains, the sparrows also used to eat worms and insects, which prevented the loss of a major quantity of grains. Due to the absence of sparrows, the worms and insects had destroyed most of the crops.

This indicates that human intellect is limited, and man uses it to think and decide that whatever is happening is right or wrong. How can the limited comprehend the unlimited? How can the small intellect of an individual understand the infinity? We believe an incomplete event to be complete and label it as wrong, because we don't have the capacity to see the complete picture. An individual thinks with his limited intellect that he should make some improvement in the creation of God; whatever wrong God is doing, he would correct it. But when understanding of truth increases, one realizes that the exquisite manner in which everything is functioning, nobody would ever be able to operate it better.

However, all of the above explanation was from the aspect where man and God are considered to be two separate entities. But with Enquiry you have learnt who is God or Self. You yourself are the producer, director, as well as the actor (in fact all the actors) of this cosmic drama. If you think of yourself as the individual or the actor, you will never be satisfied with the story of this drama, you will always find something wrong with it, you will consider the drama to be real and suffer your character's pain as well as that of others'. You will ask, why is there so much suffering in the world if God has created this world? But if you remember that it's you in every body, everything will change. You are playing each character—positive or negative. This is your drama. You (supreme consciousness) have created this story to progress from the lowest consciousness to supreme consciousness— your original state. It's the story from supreme consciousness to supreme consciousness.

Also remember that this story is progressing towards supreme consciousness because many of you are gaining wisdom and remembering the truth. You are realizing who you are and who every other being is, and therefore developing compassion for everybody and trying to raise their level of consciousness too by helping them remember their true nature.

Q. 17 : If God has created both positive and negative, then why should we always be positive and not negative?

The fundamental goal of a human being is to know oneself,

and to lift the positive, to lift the love, bliss, and stillness, that are the nature of God. In order to do so, the negative had to be created. This is because the positive cannot be understood without the negative. For example, you cannot understand love without the existence of hate. Suppose there is a completely transparent and plain glass wall. People passing by cannot see it and bump into it. Therefore something is written on the glass only for letting people know of the presence of the glass. Likewise, hatred, sorrow, anger, commotion, and heartlessness have been created so that due to these we can appreciate love, joy, peace, silence, and compassion.

It is our nature to be positive, just like the nature of water is wetness. Therefore we are not doing anybody a favor by being positive. Everything in nature—plants, birds, animals—is positive, plain, and simple.

Q. 18 : Why has God created so many human beings?

Can you tell an artist to paint just one picture, and not more? An artist will paint multiple pictures of various kinds and express himself. He will not be satisfied with just one picture. God is the artist of artists. Just by creating a few people, how will he completely demonstrate and express himself? Therefore he has created so many pictures like us to express his creativity.

Q. 19 : Why did God create this world? Why is he doing all this?

God is doing all this as a demonstration and expression of his happiness. God and happiness are one. They are not two different things. You cannot say that God is doing this for happiness, because happiness is the nature of God. God is happiness. Just as the nature of water is wetness, transparency, coolness; similarly, happiness, love, Bright silence, and creativeness are the nature of God. God is the Creator as well as the creation. God created this world because of his nature. Nobody would question an artist as to why he paints pictures. In the same way, God, like an artist, is manifesting his nature and creating the world of forms and phenomena as a demonstration of his creativity and grandeur.

Q. 20 : What is the difference between receiving the grace of God and attaining God?

Let's understand this through a story.

It was festival time and the children of a poor woman were demanding a feast. Her husband was sick and she did not have enough money to prepare a feast. But due to the relentless insistence of her children, she went to the grocery shop and explained her situation to the shopkeeper. The shopkeeper was an atheist and couldn't believe the nerve of the woman. "You expect me to give you free goodies... and what will you give me in return?" The woman politely replied that she would pray for him. The man said in a derisive tone, "Fine. Write a prayer on a piece of paper and give it to me." The woman said, "I had written a prayer just yesterday and I have that paper." She took it out of her purse and handed it over. The man dropped that paper on one side of the scale and said with a wicked smile, "I shall give you groceries equal to the weight of this prayer." He started putting items on the other side of the scale.

Something astonishing happened, which stunned everyone around. The piece of paper seemed to be so heavy that the shopkeeper went on piling groceries but the scale just wouldn't equal the weight of the paper. He could not understand how this was happening. Finally he had to give up and asked for forgiveness from the woman. He said, "I have never believed in God, but today I have experienced the power of God. Hence you can take whatever you want." The woman took the items she needed and left.

The shopkeeper couldn't stop thinking how that had happened. On a closer look, he found that the scale was broken. Now he felt even more surprised thinking how the scale which was working perfectly before the woman arrived had broken down suddenly. He picked up the piece of paper and read the prayer: "Dear God, you have given me a lot of things, now I don't want anything from you, except the understanding to recognize you."

From this story understand that the scale breaking down at the exact moment is God's grace.

Many people consider receiving the grace of God as attaining God. For example, if you receive help when needed or achieve success in your career, that's receiving God's grace. However, when people experience such grace, they think they have attained God and stop their quest for God. Some people also believe that since everything in their lives happens easily and God always helps them in some way, hence they have attained God. This is not completely correct.

It is first essential to attain knowledge about God so that you can recognize God. Arjuna received divine vision to recognize Lord Krishna and then he could see the cosmic form of the Lord. On the other hand, we don't receive any divine vision and see the actor playing the role of Lord Krishna on the television and believe it to be the real thing. Whatever vision the director comes up with regarding the form of Lord Krishna, the viewers consider it to be true. That is why it is essential to know what is that divine vision, what is that supreme knowledge, to recognize God? This will help you to attain God.

Receiving a human body and the presence of breath in it is a huge grace of God. But people don't feel that it's grace. However, if someone who is on the brink of death is asked whether breathing is grace, he will definitely agree. Healthy people do not even think about the breath and never regard it as grace. Most people's definition of grace is: "I should achieve success and a lot of wealth." But if you ask people who already have a lot of wealth whether they have been showered with God's grace, they will tell you something else.

The fact is God's grace has already been bestowed upon all people because attaining a human birth is grace. If a newborn baby does not breathe, everybody holds their breath and wait for the baby to breathe. This means they feel grace when the baby breathes and cries.

All the above examples illustrate that receiving God's grace and attaining God are two different things. You attain a true guru by God's grace and you become the true guru (the Self or God) by attaining God (Self realization and stabilization).

Q. 21 : Is it necessary to fear God? Does God get angry?

It is totally unnecessary to fear God. It is because of our assumptions about God that fear was created. Fear of God was used by society to ensure that virtuous deeds are performed by people. However, virtuous deeds performed out of fear of God are useless. Virtuous deeds should be done, not out of fear, but out of respect, love, reverence, and understanding of God.

The meaning of *God* itself is love and *love* can never be displeased. Man wrongly believes that if he happens to pass by a temple and forgets to join his hands in worship, then God gets displeased or angry with him. Man thinks that God is just like him. If God too gets angry, then what is the difference between God and man? In a lighter vein, one can say that God does get angry with the fact that man thinks that God gets angry.

Fearing God is ignorance, praying to God is wisdom, and loving God and becoming one with God is supreme wisdom.

Q. 22 : How does one attain God?

God is already within you. When all false notions and beliefs about yourself dissolve, God manifests. Self enquiry will help you in this process by peeling away the layers of false 'I's and leading you to the real 'I' (God). You can attain God not just by believing, thinking, or knowing about God, but by *being*.

Q. 23 : What is meant by false notions?

Notions are mere beliefs, which have been accepted at face value. Suppose you start believing that you are successful only when you achieve a certain set of targets in life. This means you have a false notion about success. This is because people have told you that only such an achievement is what counts as success. Now if you are unable to achieve it, you will believe that you are a failure; because the world calls it a failure. This means that unknowingly you feel that you ought to be happy or unhappy depending on the society's beliefs and concepts; whereas true happiness is something totally different.

Q. 24 : What is true happiness?

True happiness is not that happiness which you get when you achieve something. The mind has cast a shadow upon the real you. The nature of the real you is happiness. When the mind drops, then the real you (Self) that was shrouded by the mind manifests. And when that happens, you attain true happiness.

Let us suppose you have an aim or a desire to achieve something or to own something. When you actually achieve it, the mind that was consumed by that desire suddenly becomes empty for some moments because that desire has been fulfilled. In those few moments of no-mind, you experience emptiness and you feel happy. You drop into bliss, though it is just for a few minutes. All happiness you have ever experienced is only because of the mind getting empty, because of the no-mind state, because of the lifting of the shadow of the mind upon the Self. But you get the notion that happiness was the result of you attaining your desire. Due to this false notion, desire for more and newer things increases. But, anything that gives you a lot of happiness today, does not give you the same later. After some time, that happiness diminishes. On the other hand, true happiness, being your nature, is not dependent on external situations and never diminishes. We will call this as Bright happiness or *Tej* happiness to distinguish it from any other kind of happiness.

Q. 25 : How can I attain liberation from false beliefs, concepts, and notions?

Only by understanding the truth. False beliefs or notions are nothing but assumptions or concepts that the mind believes but which are not true. You believe them because you see everybody around you believing them. Thereafter you too start regarding them to be the truth. But as soon as these beliefs come under the light of understanding, they dissolve, because they actually do not exist. They are just like a thief who is hiding in the darkness, waiting for everybody to go to sleep so that he can steal. But when an alert person fetches a torch and throws light on the thief, the thief runs away. Similarly just the light of understanding is enough to permanently get rid of false beliefs. You don't need to fight anybody, nor do you need any chanting or penance to get rid of your false beliefs. Simply ask yourself, "Which beliefs do I harbor, due to which I experience sorrow?" Bring them to light and get rid of them.

Q. 26 : What are the various false beliefs that people have?

There are many false beliefs that people have, such as the belief about life and death, the belief about how to live, what clothes to wear, what is good and what is bad, the belief about religion and cults, about God and God's appearance, about fasting, penance, rituals, and so forth. These are significant false beliefs. On the other hand, there are many minor beliefs as well, such as, breaking of a mirror is a bad omen and so is a black cat crossing your path. Some consider black clothes to be inauspicious, while some believe that itching in your palms is a sign that you are going to get money. Some believe that if you laugh a lot, you will end up crying a lot. There are many such baseless beliefs that people harbor throughout the world. These are superficial beliefs. The needs of the people of every nation, geographic area, religion, and language, are different. That is why, keeping time, place, and safety in mind, everybody has created various beliefs according to what suits them. These beliefs may be minor, superficial, or even deeper beliefs.

Q. 27 : What are those deeper beliefs?

Deeper beliefs are: heaven and hell are up in the sky, we get the fruit of our deeds not in this life but in the next life, God gets angry, people are bad, time and money is limited, I am Hindu or Muslim or Christian or Jew, I am a male or a female, I am white or black or brown, and so forth. However, the deepest and the biggest false belief is believing yourself to be the body.

All false beliefs that you harbor are like a cage, they encage you and hence it is essential to break free from them. Only then can you attain true happiness. You need to attain understanding of the truth to achieve freedom from beliefs. Understanding is the key to the cage of beliefs. The belief 'I am the body' is the root of the tree of beliefs. When this root is chopped with enquiry, the entire tree collapses and you realize your true self.

Q. 28 : How do we get rid of anger, depression, greed, ego, etc.?

First things first. First find out, "Who am I?" Who is it that gets angry or depressed? Are you the one who is troubled or is it your mind? Is it you who is ill or is it your body? First get rid of false notions, then all such things such as anger, depression, greed, ego, etc. will automatically vanish.

You may have heard the story of Dushyant and Shankuntala which is written by the great Sanskrit poet Kalidasa. Suppose your friend Ramdas is enacting the role of Shakuntala on stage. You go to watch the play. You know your friend Ramdas very well. After the play is over, you meet him backstage. You are shocked to see that he is still immersed in that role and believes himself to be Shakuntala. He is unable to detach himself from the role. He is still agitated about being separated from her husband. He asks you, "When will this suffering end? When will I get to meet my husband? Will I be alone forever?"

What will you do? You will try to pull him out of his stupor. You will tell him that his problems are all due to his assumed identity. You will remind him that he is not the lady Shakuntala. It was only a role that he was enacting. As the role no longer exists, the sorrow is baseless. You will ask him to enquire who he truly is. When he realizes his true identity, the illusion of being Shakuntala will vanish.

There are deep hints hidden in the above example. Ramdas signifies the real you who has forgotten your true identity after coming to Earth. You get the same advice, which Ramdas got, from your Guru in your real life. Man plays various roles in his drama of life. He gets so attached to those roles that he forgets his real identity. Even when he approaches his Guru, he assumes himself to be one of the characters and asks the remedy for his problems and sufferings. The Guru advices him to enquire who he truly is and his suffering will then instantaneously vanish.

Initially man fails to understand these things. But when he keeps faith and contemplates upon the teachings of his Guru, the thirst for the ultimate truth awakens within him. This brings about a change in his questions. His prayers also change. Then he asks the Guru when he will attain enlightenment. The Guru says, "The one who seeks enlightenment (i.e. the false you) will never attain it. When the illusory identity vanishes, the state of enlightenment is automatically revealed." When one begins to understand this truth, it dents the shell of ignorance. Then he honestly questions himself, "Am I really this body-mind? Am I the role that I am enacting? If I am none of these, then who am I?"

In this way, when one begins to seriously doubt one's own identity, then one can make progress on the path of truth. Until then, Shakuntala (the ego) will keep cribbing and asking Kalidasa (God), "Why can't my story be a little better than what it is now?" In fact, she will blame Kalidasa for her fate. Man often does the same. Without understanding his true nature, he doubts God. He fails to understand the divine cosmic play which is being enacted and gets disappointed with God. He holds God responsible for his misfortune.

Until you realize your true nature, there will be no end to your grievances. As you realize your essence, you will begin to comprehend the cosmic drama. Then the hidden secrets of this worldly play will unfold before you.

• • •

Editor's Note: The Magic of Awakening Retreat mentioned in Appendix-II, which is based on Sirshree's teachings and conducted by Tej Gyan Foundation, will help you to realize your true self by listening to the truth. Also books by Sirshree are available on various topics and various paths, that will help you to understand the truth.

APPENDIX - II

ABOUT SIRSHREE

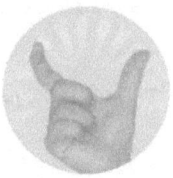

Symbol of Acceptance

Sirshree's spiritual quest which began during his childhood, led him on a journey through various schools of thought and meditation practices. The over powering desire to attain the truth made him relinquish his teaching job. After a long period of contemplation, his spiritual quest culminated in the attainment of the ultimate truth. Sirshree says, "All paths that lead to the truth begin differently, but end in the same way—with understanding. Understanding is the whole thing. Listening to this understanding is enough to attain the truth."

This understanding begins with the *mantra* of acceptance. The mantra of acceptance is: 'Can I accept this?' symbolized by the *mudra* (gesture) portrayed above. Sirshree espouses that the understanding of truth is beyond personalities. Seekers of truth need to go beyond personality-worship and embrace the formless truth. Hence, instead of using photographs, the symbol of acceptance is used to represent Sirshree.

To disseminate the understanding of truth, Sirshree devised Tejgyan—a unique system for wisdom—that helps one to progress from self-help to self-realization. He has delivered more than 2500 discourses and written over 100 books. His books have been translated in more than ten languages and published by leading publishers such as Penguin Books, Hay House Publishers, Jaico Books, Yogi Impressions, etc. Sirshree's retreats have transformed the lives of thousands and his teachings have inspired various social initiatives for raising global consciousness.

TEJ GYAN... THE ROAD AHEAD

What is Tejgyan?

Tejgyan is the existential wisdom of the ultimate truth, which is beyond duality. In today's world, there are a lot of people who feel disharmony and are desperately trying to achieve some balance in an unpredictable life. Tejgyan helps them in harmonizing with their true nature, the Self, thereby restoring balance in all aspects of their life.

And then there are those who are successful but feel a sense of emptiness or void within. Tejgyan provides them fulfillment and helps them to embark on a journey towards self-realization. There are others who feel lost and are seeking the meaning of life. Tejgyan helps them to realize the true purpose of human life.

All this is possible with Tejgyan due to a very simple reason. The experience of the ultimate truth is always available. The direct experience of this truth or self-realization is possible provided the right method is known. Tejgyan is that method, that understanding. At Tej Gyan Foundation, Sirshree imparts this understanding through a System for Wisdom – a series of retreats that guides participants step by step.

Magic of Awakening Retreat (M.A. Retreat)

Magic of Awakening is the flagship self-realization retreat offered by Tej Gyan Foundation where participants gain access to the experience of the Self and learn to live in the present every moment. The retreat is conducted in two languages – Hindi and English. The teachings of the retreat are non-denominational (secular).

Participate in the *Magic of Awakening* retreat to attain the ageless wisdom through a unique and simple 'System for Wisdom' so that you can:

1. Live from pure and still presence allowing the natural qualities of Consciousness, viz. peace, love, joy, compassion, abundance and creativity to manifest.

2. Acquire simple tools to use in everyday life which help quieten the chattering mind, revealing your true nature.

3. Get practical techniques to gain access to pure presence at will and connect to the source of all answers (the inner guru).

4. Discover the missing links in the practices of meditation *(dhyana)*, action *(karma)*, wisdom *(gyana)* and devotion *(bhakti)*.

5. Understand the nature of your body-mind mechanism to attain freedom from tendencies and patterns.

6. Learn practical methods to shift from mind-centred living to consciousness-centred living.

This residential retreat is held for 3-5 days at the foundation's MaNaN Ashram amidst the glory of mountains and the pristine beauty of nature. This ashram is located at the outskirts of the city of Pune in India, and is well connected by air, road and rail. The retreat is also held at other centres of Tej Gyan Foundation across the world.

For retreats in English email: ma@tejgyan.com

For retreats in Hindi, contact +91 9921008060 or email mail@tejgyan.com

A Mini retreat is also conducted, especially for teens (14-17 years) during summer and winter vacations.

You can now register online for all the above retreats at www.tejgyan.org

MaNaN Ashram :

Survey No. 43, Sanas Nagar, Nandoshi gaon, Kirkatwadi Phata, Sinhagad Road, Tal. Haveli, Dist. Pune 411024, Maharashtra, India. Contact No.: 992100 8060.

About Tej Gyan Foundation

Tej Gyan Foundation (TGF) was established with the mission of creating a highly evolved society through all-round self development of every individual that transforms all the facets of his/her life. It is a non-profit organization founded on the teachings of Sirshree. The foundation has received the ISO Certification (ISO 9001:2008) for its system of imparting wisdom. It has centres all across India as well as in other countries. The motto of Tej Gyan Foundation is 'Happy Thoughts'.

TGF is creating a highly evolved society through:

- Tejgyan Programs (Retreats, Courses, Television and Radio Programs, Podcasts)
- Tejgyan Products (Books, Tapes, Audio/Video CDs)
- Tejgyan Projects (Value Education, Women Empowerment, Peace Initiatives)

The foundation undertakes various projects to elevate the level of consciousness among school students, youth, women, senior citizens, teachers, doctors, leaders, organizations, police force, prisoners, etc.

❖ ❖ ❖

Books can be delivered at your doorstep by registered post or courier. You can request for the same through postal money order or pay by VPP. Please send the money order to either of the following two addresses:

WOW Publishings Pvt. Ltd.

1. Registered Office: E-4, Vaibhav Nagar, Near Tapovan Mandir, Pimpri, Pune 411017.

2. Post Box No. 36, Pimpri Colony Post Office, Pimpri, Pune 411017.

Phone No. : 09011013210 / 9623457873

YOU CAN ALSO ORDER YOUR COPY AT THE ONLINE STORE:

Log in at: www.gethappythoughts.org

*Postage fee will not be charged when you order books by post.

**Plus 10% Discount on purchases above Rs. 300/-.

OTHER BOOKS BY SIRSHREE

ISBN : 978-81-906627-6-5

Total Pages 240

WOW Publishings Pvt. Ltd.

COMPLETE MEDITATION
From doing Meditation to being Meditation

This book is the most comprehensive book on meditation which guides you on the path of meditation, whether you are a beginner, a seeker, a disciple or a devotee. It answers questions according to the level of the seeker at each stage. It systematically explains the methods and techniques of meditation which benefit you in every aspect of life. It ultimately reveals that meditation is our true nature and takes you on a journey of spiritual evolution from doing meditation to being meditation. It shows how meditation not only helps to release stress, but is a path to attain supreme consciousness.

ISBN : 978-81-8415-627-0

Total Pages 72

WOW Publishings Pvt Ltd

ANSWERS THAT AWAKEN
Access the Source of Wisdom within You

Spirituality in its true form is neither an escape nor refuge. It's about reconnecting with our real self, realizing our hidden potential, preparing ourselves to deal with emerging situations and much, much more. Until we remove the blindfold of ignorance and understand the real truth about life and living, we'll continue to believe fallacies and get bogged down by existential dilemmas. The truth of life lies in the art of being one with life – a truth that not only takes us forward in our spiritual quest, but also elevates our level of consciousness.

This book is a select compilation of profound answers that arise from the quintessence of wisdom. These answers unravel the deepest truths about life and living, which dissolve existential dilemmas and reveal the essence of spirituality.

For further details contact:

TEJ GYAN FOUNDATION

Registered Office :

Happy Thoughts Building, Vikrant Complex, Near Tapovan Mandir, Pimpri, Pune 411017, Maharashtra, India.

Contact No.: 020-27411240, 27412576

Email: mail@tejgyan.com

MaNaN Ashram :

Survey No. 43, Sanas Nagar, Nandoshi gaon, Kirkatwadi Phata, Sinhagad Road, Tal. Haveli, Dist. Pune 411024, Maharashtra, India. Contact No.: 99210 08060.

Hyderabad: 9885558100, **Bangalore**: 09880412588,
Delhi: 9891059875, **Nashik**: 9326967980, **Mumbai**: 9373440985

For accessing our unique 'System for Wisdom' from Self-help to Self-realization, please follow us on:

	Website	www.tejgyan.org
	Video Channel	www.youtube.com/tejgyan
	Social networking	www.facebook.com/tejgyan
	Social networking	www.twitter.com/sirshree
	Internet Radio	http://www.tejgyan.org internetradio.aspx

Online shopping
www.gethappythoughts.org

Watch Sirshree on

SANSKAR TV CHANNEL

Mon to Sat 6:35 - 6:55 p.m.,
Sun 8:10 - 8:30 p.m.

(These timings may be subject to change.)

U R Meditation App
A new way to meditate

Now available in English/Hindi

Free Meditation App to download meditations

World Peace Initiative

Please pray for World Peace along with thousands of others at 09:09 a.m. and p.m. every day.

www.ingramcontent.com/pod-product-compliance
Lightning Source LLC
LaVergne TN
LVHW040149080526
838202LV00042B/3083